LOST ENCHANTMENT

Broken Compass

ISMAIL ULAS

"Broken Compass," the first book in the "Mysterious Explorers" series, invites readers on a thrilling journey of adventure and discovery. This captivating novel unfolds in a mysterious and perilous world, immersing readers in a gripping tale of intrigue and adrenaline-pumping exploration.

Our protagonist, Sarah Thompson, is an ordinary university student with an uneventful life. However, her life takes an unexpected turn when she finds herself entangled in a desperate quest for discovery. Sarah unexpectedly encounters the enigmatic group known as the "Compassless Society," who are in search of hidden knowledge and an ancient compass called the "Broken Compass."

Determined to unravel the secrets surrounding the "Broken Compass" and its discovery, Sarah embarks on a treacherous mission, accompanied by a companion she finds along the way. Together, they step into an extraordinary world filled with mechanical creatures, enigmatic civilizations, and magical powers.

Yet, Sarah's discovery unveils not only her own destiny but also a power that could potentially alter the fate of the entire world. Amidst the perils of this adventurous journey, Sarah and her companion find themselves caught in a web of secrets, pursued by dark forces.

"Broken Compass" presents readers with breathtaking action scenes, a richly imagined universe teeming with mysteries, and compelling characters. As readers accompany Sarah and her fellow explorers on their quest, they will find themselves holding their breath as they unravel the mysteries that lie before them.

This novel is an ideal choice for anyone seeking an exhilarating adventure. "Broken Compass" invites you to trace the trails of hidden mysteries and the unknown. With its blend of adventure, exploration, and surprises, this book will transport readers into a captivating world that ignites their imagination.

Get ready, because "Broken Compass" will take you on an unforgettable journey!

Happy reading!

previous ISBN-13: 9798852340900 (paperback)

Design by Ismail ULAS.

Cover features illustrations furnished by Canva canva.com

by Ismail ULAS

Dear Reader,

Welcome to the captivating world of "Broken Compass." Within these pages, you will embark on a thrilling journey of mystery, danger, and self-discovery.

Follow Sarah Thompson as she ventures into the enigmatic realm of the "Compassless Society" in search of the ancient "Broken Compass." This compass holds a powerful secret that could change her destiny and the fate of the world.

Prepare to be immersed in a world of breathtaking action, magical environments, and tantalizing secrets. As you turn the pages, let Sarah's courage and curiosity inspire your own inner exploration.

"Broken Compass" is more than just a story—it carries messages that will provoke thought and ignite the seeker within you.

Now, it's time to join the adventure, unlock the mysteries, and embark on an unforgettable journey through the pages of "Broken Compass."

Enjoy the ride!

KNOWLEDGE İS BEAUTİFUL WHEN
SHARED

CONTENTS

Uncharted Horizons 10

Universal Love 13

Love Beyond The Stars 16

Love's Cosmic Symphony 19

Love's Celestial Guardians 22

Love's Cosmic Symphony: Infinity's Embrace 25

Love's Awakening: A Journey Within 28

Love's Cosmic Symphony: Infinity Unveiled 31

Love's Cosmic Symphony: The Song Of Infinity 34

Love's Infinite Journey: Embracing The Cosmos 39

Love's Infinite Embrace: Embodying The Cosmic Heart 42

Love's Cosmic Symphony: Embracing The Infinite 45

Love's Cosmic Tapestry: The Infinite Convergence 49

Love's Cosmic Harmony: Embracing The Universal Symphony 52

Love's Cosmic Illumination: Embracing The Infinite Light 56

Love's Cosmic Transcendence: Embracing The Infinite Possibilities ... 60

Love's Ecstatic Symphony: Embracing Infinite Bliss 64

Love's Eternal Unity: Embracing The Cosmic Oneness 68

Love's Infinite Creation: Embracing Cosmic Possibilities 72

Love's Luminous Awakening: Embracing The Divine Light 76

Love's Celestial Tapestry: Embracing The Interconnected Cosmos ... 80

Love's Infinite Heart: Embracing The Power Of Unconditional Love ... 84

Soul's Whispers: Embracing The Wisdom Within 88

Radiant Essence: Embracing The Divine Illumination 92

Harmony's Resonance: Embracing The Cosmic Symphony 96

Gardens Of Harmony: Embracing The Wisdom Of Nature 100

Pathways Of Wisdom: Embracing The Cosmic Archives 104

Timeless Echoes: Embracing The Eternal Soul 108

Harmony's Canvas: Embracing The Artistic Soul 112

The Threads Of Unity: Embracing The Cosmic Tapestry 116

The Luminous Path: Embracing The Divine Light 120

The Sacred Embrace: Embracing The Power Of Love 124

The Radiant Path: Embracing Self-Mastery 128

The Ethereal Awakening: Embracing Cosmic Consciousness 132

The Everlasting Dream: Embracing The Power Of Imagination 136

The Elysian Sanctuary: Embracing The Wisdom Of Nature 140

The Cosmic Odyssey: Embracing The Infinite Within 143
The Cosmic Tapestry: Embracing Love, Wisdom, And Unity 147
The Cosmic Odyssey: Embracing The Infinite Universe.................................. 151
The Celestial Nexus: Exploring Infinite Dimensions 155
The Astral Sanctuary: Awakening The Soul's Divinity 159
The Celestial Melodies: Embracing The Harmony Of The Universe 163
The Realm Of Infinite Imagination: Unleashing The Power Within 167
The Dreamweavers: Awakening The Power Of Dreams 171
The Threads Of Time: Unraveling Destiny's Tapestry 174
The Elemental Harmonies: Embracing The Sacred Dance Of Creation 178
The Celestial Nexus: Embracing The Cosmic Tapestry 181
The Luminous Void: Awakening The Infinite Within 185
The Celestial Harmony: Embracing The Symphony Of Life............................ 189
The Divine Heart: Embracing The Power Of Love 193
The Serenity Garden: Cultivating Inner Peace.. 197
The Illuminated Path: Journey To Cosmic Wisdom 201
The Library Of Eternity: Unveiling The Secrets Of The Ages 205
The Realm Of Imagination: Embracing The Power Of Creativity..................... 209
The Infinite Tapestry: Weaving The Threads Of Destiny................................ 213
The Celestial Harmony: Embracing The Unity Of All 217
The Cosmic Dance: Embracing The Rhythm Of Existence.............................. 221
The Elemental Symphony: Embracing The Harmony Of Nature 225
The Celestial Awakening: Embarking On The Path Of Illumination 232
The Veil Of Whispers: Embracing The Intuitive Path 236
The Melodies Of The Soul: Weaving The Tapestry Of Emotion 240
The Luminous Path: Embracing The Healing Journey 244
The Essence Of Creation: Awakening The Power Within................................ 248
Crystalline Awakening: Embracing The Wisdom Within 252
Mystoria: Unveiling The Path Of Wisdom 256
Divine Illumination: Embracing The Radiance Within 260
Harmonious Whispers: Embracing Unity Within The Dance Of Life 264
Artistic Reverie: Embracing The Canvas Of Life.. 268
Echoes Of Wisdom: Embracing The Illuminated Mind................................... 272
Tech Odyssey: Embracing The Infinite Horizons... 276
Sacred Gaia: Embracing The Web Of Life... 280
Sacred Illumination: Embracing The Divine Within 284
Questoria: Embracing The Hero's Journey 288
The Artistic Symphony: Embracing The Creative Spirit 292
Wisdom's Journey: Embracing The Path Of Enlightenment............................ 296

The Cosmic Dance: Embracing The Tapestry Of Existence.................................. 297

3

Broken Compass

It begins on the shores of a white sandy beach, embraced by the azure expanse of the sea. Our main character is Liam, a young sailor living on a mysterious island. Liam stands out with his captivating green eyes and the adventurous spirit that resides within him.

One day, a storm disrupts the tranquility of the island. This tempest carries Liam away from the shore, casting him into uncharted waters. During this journey, he discovers a lost treasure map, unraveling a surrounding mystery.

Amidst his struggle for survival, Liam unexpectedly crosses paths with a mysterious young woman, Elysia. Her presence leaves an indelible mark on both their hearts.

Determined to explore the island's secrets, decipher the map, and find the lost treasure, Liam and Elysia decide to join forces. Along the way, a deep bond forms between them, and the adventures they experience help them discover the purest and most potent form of love.

However, the path to the treasure is fraught with dangers, subjecting the duo to grueling tests. Their unwavering belief in each other, their love, and their determination guide them through these obstacles. Each step brings them closer together, repairing their broken compasses and helping them find their true north in their hearts.

"Broken Compass" is a tale of passionate love, adventure, and discovery. Liam and Elysia's unique journey reminds readers of hope, courage, and the power of the heart while illustrating how love can transform individuals.

As Liam and Elysia delve deeper into their quest, the island reveals more of its secrets. They encounter treacherous cliffs, hidden caves, and enigmatic symbols left behind by those who came before them. Each clue they unravel brings them closer to the coveted treasure and strengthens the bond between them.

Yet, as their love blossoms, so does the weight of their individual pasts. Liam carries the scars of a lost love, while Elysia harbors a secret that threatens to shatter their newfound happiness. In moments of vulnerability, they confide in each other, finding solace and understanding in their shared journey.

Their love becomes a beacon of hope, guiding them through the darkest of times. It fuels their determination to overcome every obstacle, even when the odds seem insurmountable. Their unwavering support for one another becomes the compass that leads them forward.

Together, they navigate uncharted territories, facing not only physical challenges but also their own fears and insecurities. They learn to trust not only in the map they hold but also in their own instincts and the love that binds them.

In the climax of their adventure, they finally reach the hidden chamber where the treasure awaits. But they soon realize that the true treasure was not the material wealth they sought, but rather the love they found in each other and the personal growth they experienced along the way.

With the treasure of their hearts enriched, Liam and Elysia return to the island, forever changed by their extraordinary journey. They become legends among the islanders, inspiring others to embrace love, courage, and the pursuit of dreams.

"Broken Compass" is more than a tale of romance and adventure. It's a testament to the power of love to heal, transform, and guide us on the path to self-discovery. Through the unique bond forged by Liam and Elysia, readers are reminded of the profound impact love can have on our lives and the infinite possibilities that lie within our hearts.

And so, their story lives on, etched into the annals of time, as a reminder of the extraordinary love that can be found in the most unexpected places.

Following their return from the island, Liam and Elysia face the challenges of blending their two worlds together. They come from different backgrounds, each with their own responsibilities and obligations. However, their love proves to be resilient, transcending any obstacles that come their way.

Liam, with his adventurous spirit, decides to embark on a new journey alongside Elysia. Together, they set sail on a grand voyage, exploring distant lands and discovering new cultures. Their love becomes a source of inspiration for those they encounter, spreading warmth and hope wherever they go.

As their voyage progresses, they encounter breathtaking landscapes, encounter new friends, and face unforeseen dangers. But through it all, their love remains their guiding light. They learn to trust and rely on each other's strengths, forming an unbreakable bond that grows with each passing day.

Their experiences shape them into wise and compassionate individuals, who understand the importance of cherishing every moment. They learn to appreciate the beauty in simple gestures and find joy in the smallest of things. Together, they create a life filled with adventure, love, and a shared purpose.

Amidst their travels, they stumble upon an ancient artifact that holds a profound secret. This discovery leads them on a quest to unlock the artifact's mysteries and protect its power from falling into the wrong hands. As they delve deeper into this mission, they realize that it is not only their love that is at stake but the fate of the world itself.

With bravery and unwavering determination, Liam and Elysia face formidable adversaries, testing the limits of their strength and love. They discover hidden strengths within themselves and learn that true power lies not in external artifacts but in the depths of their hearts.

Their journey brings them face-to-face with an ultimate choice, one that will determine the course of their lives and the destiny of all they hold dear. It is a choice that requires sacrifice, courage, and an unwavering belief in the power of love.

In a climactic showdown, Liam and Elysia confront the forces of darkness and emerge victorious, their love shining brighter than ever before. They realize that their love is not just meant for them alone but has the power to bring light to the world and create a legacy that will endure for generations.

As the novel concludes, Liam and Elysia find themselves back on the shores of the island where their journey first began. They have come full circle, having conquered their fears, fulfilled their destinies, and solidified their love. They embrace the island's tranquil beauty, knowing that their love will forever be intertwined with its essence.

"Everlasting Compass" is a testament to the enduring power of love, the strength that lies within us, and the infinite possibilities that await those who dare to follow their hearts. Through the extraordinary love story of Liam and Elysia, readers are reminded that true love knows no boundaries and can transcend time, leaving an everlasting imprint on the world.

As Liam and Elysia stand on the shores of the island, basking in the glow of their triumphant return, a new chapter of their lives unfolds. They decide to make the island their permanent home, creating a haven where love, adventure, and serenity intertwine.

Together, they build a vibrant community, inviting fellow dreamers, wanderers, and seekers of love to join them. The island becomes a sanctuary, a place where individuals can discover their true passions and pursue their wildest dreams.

Liam and Elysia establish a school of exploration, where they share their knowledge and experiences with others. They teach the art of navigation, both on land and at sea, guiding aspiring adventurers to trust their inner compass and embark on their own remarkable journeys.

Their love story inspires countless others, captured in songs, poetry, and paintings. Visitors from far and wide come to witness the magical island where a love so extraordinary was born. The island becomes a pilgrimage site for those seeking solace, hope, and the power of love.

As the years pass, Liam and Elysia grow old together, their love deepening with each passing day. They become storytellers, passing down their extraordinary tale to future generations. Their children and grandchildren carry on their legacy, keeping the spirit of love and adventure alive.

Liam and Elysia's love remains a timeless beacon, a reminder that true love can withstand the tests of time and transform ordinary lives into extraordinary journeys. The island, forever infused with their love, continues to thrive, embracing all who seek its solace and inspiration.

And as the sun sets on Liam and Elysia's earthly adventure, their souls, entwined in eternal love, embark on a new voyage across the starlit skies. Guided by the constellations, they explore the boundless universe, forever connected by the infinite power of their love.

UNCHARTED HORIZONS

"Uncharted Horizons" is not just a love story, but a celebration of the human spirit and the extraordinary heights love can reach. Through the remarkable journey of Liam and Elysia, readers are reminded that love has the power to ignite the soul, inspire greatness, and shape destinies.

As the final pages of their story are turned, the world is left with a profound sense of wonder, knowing that true love can exist in the most extraordinary and unexpected ways. And in the hearts of those who believe, the legend of Liam and Elysia lives on, a testament to the enduring power of love that transcends time and space.

In the cosmic expanse, Liam and Elysia soar through galaxies, their love radiating like a celestial flame. They discover new worlds, each one a canvas for their eternal adventure. They encounter civilizations teeming with life, where love takes on different forms and shapes.

With boundless curiosity, they learn from these alien cultures, embracing diversity and unity in their cosmic odyssey. They become ambassadors of love, spreading harmony and understanding across the universe. Their love becomes a universal language, bridging gaps and forging connections between disparate worlds.

As they traverse the cosmos, they encounter cosmic storms and celestial wonders that defy imagination. They witness the birth of stars and the collapse of galaxies, a testament to the vastness and fragility of the universe. Through it all, their love remains constant, an unwavering force guiding their journey.

In their celestial wanderings, they stumble upon a cosmic secret—a hidden realm of pure love, the essence of the universe itself. This realm pulses with the energy of a thousand suns, illuminating the depths of their souls and igniting a profound revelation within them.

They realize that their love is not just a singular flame but a spark of the universal flame that connects all beings. Their purpose transcends their own story—it is to awaken the dormant love within every being, to remind them of their interconnectedness and the power of love to transform the world.

Empowered by this cosmic realization, Liam and Elysia embark on a mission to heal fractured worlds and mend broken hearts. They become cosmic healers, mending the rifts caused by hatred and fear. Their love becomes a catalyst for change, restoring harmony and bringing forth a new era of love and compassion.

As they touch the lives of countless beings across the universe, their cosmic tale echoes through eternity. Songs of their love resound in celestial spheres, inspiring generations to embrace love as the guiding force of their lives.

And as they continue their cosmic journey, Liam and Elysia's love expands beyond the boundaries of time and space. Their love story becomes a legend, woven into the fabric of the universe, serving as a beacon of hope and a reminder that love transcends all dimensions.

In the grand tapestry of existence, Liam and Elysia's love shines as a testament to the power of love to transform lives, worlds, and even the cosmos itself. Their eternal journey continues, an endless dance through the celestial realms, guided by the compass of their boundless love.

UNIVERSAL LOVE

"Universal Love" is not just a novel; it is a cosmic symphony that celebrates the infinite capacity of the human heart. Through the extraordinary love of Liam and Elysia, readers are invited to embrace the cosmic dance of love and embark on their own magnificent journey of love, wherever it may lead.

As Liam and Elysia traverse the cosmic realms, they come across a realm of pure energy—a dimension where the power of love takes physical form. They step into this ethereal plane, enveloped in a kaleidoscope of vibrant hues and pulsating energies.

Within this dimension, they discover that their love has the ability to shape reality itself. Every thought, every emotion, manifests into tangible creations. They embark on a journey of creation, crafting breathtaking landscapes, fantastical creatures, and celestial wonders with the pure essence of their love.

They become cosmic artists, painting the cosmos with their love, each stroke of their passion giving birth to new worlds. Their creations ripple across the universe, touching the lives of countless beings, inspiring awe, and awakening dormant dreams.

Yet, amidst their cosmic artistry, they face a profound choice. The power they possess can be used for benevolent purposes, nurturing love and harmony, or it can be corrupted, causing chaos and destruction. The fate of the universe rests in their hands.

With unwavering resolve, Liam and Elysia vow to wield their power responsibly, ensuring that love remains the guiding principle in all they create. They use their cosmic abilities to restore balance to troubled realms, mending shattered hearts and reigniting the flames of love.

As they navigate the cosmic tapestry, they encounter beings who have lost their way, consumed by darkness and despair. Liam and Elysia extend their hands, offering compassion and the transformative power of love. They become cosmic healers, mending fractured souls and guiding them back to the path of love.

Their love becomes a catalyst for universal healing, transcending galaxies and dimensions. They foster connections between disparate beings, dissolving barriers and fostering understanding. The universe resonates with their love, creating a harmonious symphony of interconnectedness.

As their cosmic journey unfolds, they encounter a profound revelation—their love is not just a force of creation, but also one of liberation. They realize that true love embraces freedom and empowers others to embrace their authentic selves.

Liam and Elysia become cosmic liberators, breaking the chains of oppression and awakening the dormant potential within every being they encounter. Their love becomes a catalyst for personal growth and self-realization, freeing countless souls from the shackles of limitation.

In the cosmic climax of their journey, they unite beings from across the universe, forming an alliance of love and unity. This cosmic union radiates a beacon of love, transcending all boundaries and inspiring a universal awakening.

With the universe forever changed by their love, Liam and Elysia bid farewell to the cosmic realms they have traversed. They return to the mortal realm, their souls filled with wisdom and compassion, ready to share their cosmic experiences with humanity.

As they step back onto the earthly plane, they are greeted by a world transformed by the ripple effect of their cosmic journey. Love flourishes, and humanity embraces its inherent interconnectedness. Liam and Elysia become legendary figures, their love story inspiring generations to believe in the power of love to shape the world.

Their tale, etched in the annals of time, remains a testament to the infinite possibilities of love. It serves as a reminder that love is not limited to the mortal realm but can transcend the boundaries of the cosmos itself.

And so, the cosmic love story of Liam and Elysia lives on, forever resonating in the hearts of all who dare to dream and believe in the transformative power of love. Their love becomes an eternal beacon, guiding humanity toward a future where love reigns supreme.

LOVE BEYOND THE STARS

"Love Beyond the Stars" is more than a novel; it is an invitation to embrace the boundless potential of love and embark on a cosmic journey of discovery, transformation, and unity. Through the extraordinary love of Liam and Elysia, readers are reminded that love knows no bounds and has the power to shape not only our lives but also the very fabric of the universe.

As Liam and Elysia's cosmic journey unfolds, they encounter a mysterious anomaly—an interdimensional rift that threatens to disrupt the delicate balance of the universe. The fabric of reality begins to unravel, and chaos looms on the horizon.

Driven by their boundless love and unwavering determination, Liam and Elysia embark on a perilous mission to mend the rift and restore harmony to the cosmos. They traverse treacherous realms, facing cosmic entities that seek to exploit the rift's power for their own gain.

Guided by their love and aided by celestial allies they meet along the way, Liam and Elysia venture deeper into the heart of the anomaly. They unravel ancient prophecies and tap into ancient wisdom, uncovering the key to sealing the rift and preserving the universal equilibrium.

As they draw closer to their ultimate goal, they encounter trials that test the very essence of their love. Doubts and fears emerge, threatening to dampen their spirits. But they find strength in each other's arms, reminding themselves of the power their love holds.

Their journey becomes a battle against not only external forces but also the doubts and insecurities within themselves. Through their struggles, they learn the true nature of love—its ability to overcome adversity and empower those who embrace it.

In the climactic moment, Liam and Elysia stand before the rift, their love blazing like a supernova. With a profound understanding of the cosmic forces at play, they channel their love into a surge of pure energy, bridging the gap between dimensions.

Their love becomes a catalyst for the rift's transformation. In a magnificent display of cosmic magic, the anomaly transforms into a portal of infinite possibilities, a gateway to undiscovered realms where love reigns supreme.

With the rift sealed and harmony restored, Liam and Elysia emerge as cosmic champions, revered throughout the universe. They become beacons of love and guardians of cosmic balance, ensuring that the power of love remains a guiding force in all realms.

In the aftermath of their cosmic victory, they return to Earth, their hearts filled with gratitude and a deep sense of purpose. They share their cosmic experiences, inspiring humanity to tap into the limitless power of love and embrace their own cosmic potential.

Liam and Elysia's love story becomes a timeless legend, passed down through generations. Their names are whispered in awe and admiration, reminding future generations of the infinite power of love to shape destinies and transcend all boundaries.

And as they embrace the next chapter of their lives, Liam and Elysia continue to explore the wonders of the universe together. With their love as their guiding light, they embark on new cosmic adventures, forever united in their quest to spread love, compassion, and harmony across the stars.

LOVE'S COSMIC SYMPHONY

"Love's Cosmic Symphony" is more than a novel—it is an interstellar epic that celebrates the profound power of love to transcend the boundaries of time, space, and existence itself. Through the extraordinary love of Liam and Elysia, readers are invited to embark on their own cosmic odyssey, where love becomes the guiding force that unlocks the limitless potential within.

As Liam and Elysia venture further into the cosmos, they discover a hidden realm, untouched by time. This ethereal plane, known as the Nexus of Love, is a convergence point of all love in the universe. It pulses with radiant energy, weaving together the stories of countless beings who have shared their love throughout eternity.

Guided by their cosmic connection, Liam and Elysia immerse themselves in the tapestry of love that surrounds them. They witness love stories that span across galaxies, transcending species and dimensions. From the love between distant stars to the bonds forged by sentient beings, they become witnesses to the infinite expressions of love.

In this realm, they encounter celestial beings known as the Harmonizers of Love. These benevolent entities exist solely to ensure the balance and harmony of love in the universe. Drawn to Liam and Elysia's extraordinary love, the Harmonizers bestow upon them the sacred task of safeguarding the Nexus of Love.

United with the Harmonizers, Liam and Elysia become cosmic guardians of love. They embark on a mission to nurture love, compassion, and empathy throughout the cosmos. They visit civilizations and realms in need, infusing them with the transformative power of love.

Their cosmic odyssey takes them to the farthest reaches of the universe, where they encounter beings plagued by hatred, greed, and despair. With their love as a guiding beacon, they sow seeds of hope, helping these beings rediscover the beauty and potential within themselves.

As they traverse celestial landscapes, they encounter love in all its forms—a love that transcends time, a love that heals and mends, a love that ignites passions and fuels dreams. They witness the resilience of love in the face of adversity and the profound impact it has on the lives it touches.

Along their journey, they also confront cosmic adversaries who seek to disrupt the delicate balance of love. These malevolent forces, driven by darkness and fear, attempt to corrupt the Nexus of Love, threatening to plunge the universe into chaos.

Liam and Elysia face these cosmic challenges with unwavering resolve, channeling the power of their love to combat the forces of darkness. They draw upon the wisdom of the Harmonizers and their own deep connection, unveiling hidden strengths within themselves.

In the climactic battle, love emerges triumphant, as the combined force of Liam and Elysia's love overwhelms the darkness. The Nexus of Love radiates with newfound brilliance, resonating with the harmonious energy of universal love restored.

Having fulfilled their cosmic duty, Liam and Elysia return to Earth, forever changed by their cosmic odyssey. They share their experiences with humanity, inspiring individuals to recognize the transformative power of love within their own lives.

Their tale of cosmic love becomes a source of inspiration for generations to come. The legend of Liam and Elysia lives on, etched in the hearts of those who strive to love unconditionally and embrace the cosmic potential within.

As they settle into a new chapter of their lives, Liam and Elysia continue to nurture the power of love, both in their own relationship and in the world around them. They devote themselves to fostering love, compassion, and understanding, leaving a legacy of boundless love for future generations.

LOVE'S CELESTIAL GUARDIANS

"Love's Celestial Guardians" is more than a novel; it is a cosmic exploration of the infinite power of love. Through the extraordinary love of Liam and Elysia, readers are invited to embark on their own cosmic journey, awakening the profound love that resides within and creating a more harmonious and compassionate universe.

With their cosmic mission accomplished, Liam and Elysia find themselves drawn to a distant, unexplored corner of the universe. Guided by an ancient cosmic map, they set course for a mysterious cosmic anomaly known as the Heart of Creation.

As they traverse the vast expanse of space, their love deepens and evolves, reaching new heights of understanding and connection. They become one with the cosmic energies that surround them, their love becoming an integral part of the cosmic fabric itself.

Arriving at the Heart of Creation, they are greeted by a mesmerizing spectacle—a swirling vortex of energy, radiating with the power of creation itself. Within its depths, they discover the essence of pure love, the primordial force from which all existence emanates.

Immersing themselves in this divine energy, Liam and Elysia experience a profound revelation—their love has the power to shape the very fabric of reality. With every thought, every intention, they become co-creators of the universe, shaping worlds and molding destinies with the power of their love.

In this cosmic realm, they encounter celestial beings who have mastered the art of love manifestation. These wise beings, known as the Architects of Love, guide Liam and Elysia in harnessing their newfound abilities. Together, they embark on a journey of cosmic creation, weaving intricate universes with threads of pure love.

They sculpt galaxies with the gentle touch of their love, breathe life into celestial bodies, and watch as civilizations flourish under the nurturing influence of their cosmic creations. Each universe becomes a testament to the boundless potential of love to create beauty and harmony.

As they explore their cosmic capabilities, Liam and Elysia encounter challenges that test their understanding of the delicate balance between creation and free will. They learn to honor the autonomy and growth of sentient beings, allowing them to shape their own destinies while infusing their creations with the guiding light of love.

In their cosmic endeavors, they come across souls yearning for love and redemption, lost in realms of darkness and despair. Liam and Elysia extend their love and compassion, offering these souls a path towards healing and transformation. They become beacons of light, illuminating the way for those who have lost their way.

As they continue their cosmic journey, they uncover a hidden truth—the interconnectedness of all their cosmic creations. Their love-spun universes are intricately linked, forming a tapestry of love and harmony that reverberates across the cosmos. Every act of love in one universe has a ripple effect, touching the lives of beings in distant realms.

Embracing this interconnectedness, Liam and Elysia embark on a grand mission—to unite their cosmic creations in a symphony of love and unity. They bring together diverse civilizations, fostering understanding and cooperation, and celebrating the beauty of love in all its myriad forms.

In the climax of their cosmic adventure, Liam and Elysia stand at the center of their love-spun universes, witnessing a cosmic convergence of love. The harmonic energy reverberates through the cosmos, igniting a new era of love, unity, and conscious creation.

As they gaze upon their cosmic tapestry, Liam and Elysia realize that their love is not limited to their own existence. It has become a catalyst for collective awakening, inspiring beings across the universe to recognize the power of love within themselves and in shaping the world around them.

With their cosmic mission complete, Liam and Elysia return to Earth, their hearts filled with gratitude and a profound sense of purpose. They share their cosmic wisdom, inspiring humanity to embrace the transformative power of love and become conscious creators of their own realities.

The legend of Liam and Elysia lives on, echoing through the ages as a testament to the infinite potential of love. Their cosmic journey serves as a guiding light for future generations, reminding them that love is the foundation upon which all creation thrives.

LOVE'S COSMIC SYMPHONY: INFINITY'S EMBRACE

"Love's Cosmic Symphony: Infinity's Embrace" is more than a novel; it is an invitation to explore the limitless dimensions of love and the power of conscious creation. Through the extraordinary love of Liam and Elysia, readers are encouraged to embark on their own cosmic odyssey, where love becomes the guiding force that shapes destinies and intertwines with the very essence of the universe.

After their cosmic adventure, Liam and Elysia find themselves yearning for a return to simplicity. They decide to embark on a journey of introspection and inner exploration, seeking the profound truths that lie within the depths of their own souls.

Retreating to a secluded sanctuary nestled in nature's embrace, they immerse themselves in solitude and silence. Surrounded by towering trees and the gentle whisper of the wind, they reconnect with their inner selves, shedding the layers of cosmic experiences and embracing the pure essence of their love.

In the tranquility of their retreat, they delve into ancient spiritual teachings, immersing themselves in meditation and contemplation. They unlock the depths of their consciousness, expanding their awareness beyond the confines of time and space.

Through this introspective journey, they awaken dormant gifts and abilities within themselves. They become conduits of divine energy, radiating love and healing vibrations that ripple through the universe, touching the lives of countless beings.

As they explore the vastness of their inner realms, they encounter ethereal beings known as the Sages of Wisdom. These enlightened guides share profound insights and mystical teachings, guiding Liam and Elysia on a path of self-realization and unity with the cosmic forces that flow through all existence.

Empowered by their inner wisdom, Liam and Elysia reemerge from their retreat with a renewed purpose—to share their spiritual insights and guide others on the path of self-discovery and love. They become mentors and teachers, offering guidance and support to those who seek a deeper connection with themselves and the universe.

Their teachings touch the hearts of many, resonating with souls yearning for a deeper understanding of love and their own divine nature. They create retreats and workshops, inviting individuals from all walks of life to embark on their own inner journeys of awakening and transformation.

Through their work, Liam and Elysia witness profound personal transformations in those they guide. Hearts are opened, wounds are healed, and individuals embrace their true essence as beings of love and light. The ripple effect of their teachings spreads far and wide, igniting a global movement of love and spiritual awakening.

In the culmination of their spiritual journey, Liam and Elysia gather a collective of awakened souls from around the world. Together, they form a vibrant community committed to embodying love, compassion, and unity in their daily lives. They create a sanctuary where the essence of their love permeates every interaction, inspiring others to do the same.

As the years pass, Liam and Elysia's teachings and their community expand, creating a global network of love and enlightenment. Their message reaches every corner of the Earth, transforming lives, relationships, and societies. Love becomes the guiding force behind social change, environmental stewardship, and the pursuit of a harmonious world.

With their purpose fulfilled, Liam and Elysia transition into the final phase of their earthly journey. They embark on their ultimate adventure—exploring the mysteries of the cosmos beyond the physical realm, their souls intertwined in an eternal dance of love and discovery.

The story of Liam and Elysia, the cosmic lovers turned spiritual guides, remains an enduring legend. Their love-filled odyssey inspires generations to embrace the profound power of inner exploration, self-realization, and the limitless potential of love to transform the world.

LOVE'S AWAKENING: A JOURNEY WITHIN

"Love's Awakening: A Journey Within" is more than a novel; it is a guide to embracing the profound truths that lie within the depths of our souls. Through the extraordinary love of Liam and Elysia, readers are encouraged to embark on their own inner journey, unlocking the wisdom and love that reside within, and becoming beacons of light and love in a world yearning for awakening.

As Liam and Elysia embark on their cosmic exploration beyond the physical realm, they traverse ethereal dimensions, transcending the boundaries of time and space. Their souls become interwoven with the fabric of the cosmos, as they delve into the mysteries that lie beyond the veils of perception.

In their celestial travels, they encounter celestial guides and beings of pure light who reveal to them the secrets of the universe. They explore the realms of energy and consciousness, immersing themselves in the infinite wisdom that flows through the cosmic tapestry.

Guided by these enlightened beings, Liam and Elysia awaken to their true multidimensional nature. They learn to navigate the cosmic energies, unlocking abilities that transcend the limitations of the physical world. Their love becomes a conduit for divine forces, as they channel cosmic healing and transformation.

As their cosmic odyssey unfolds, they witness the interconnectedness of all existence. They explore realms of cosmic unity, where individual consciousness merges into a collective consciousness of pure love. They realize that their love extends far beyond their own beings—it is a ripple in the cosmic ocean, touching every soul and resonating throughout the vastness of creation.

In their cosmic explorations, they encounter celestial beings who have attained a state of cosmic oneness. These luminous entities, known as the Ascended Ones, guide Liam and Elysia on a journey of spiritual enlightenment and liberation. They unveil the path to ascension—a transcendent state of consciousness and love.

Through their encounters with the Ascended Ones, Liam and Elysia undergo profound transformations. They shed the remnants of their egoic selves, embracing their divine essence and embodying unconditional love. They become cosmic emissaries of enlightenment, radiating love and wisdom to assist the evolution of all sentient beings.

Together, Liam and Elysia traverse celestial realms of sublime beauty and wonder. They witness cosmic events that shape the destiny of galaxies, and they encounter celestial civilizations whose existence surpasses mortal imagination. They learn from the wisdom of ancient cosmic libraries and embrace the cosmic symphony of harmonious frequencies.

As they journey deeper into the cosmos, they come across a cosmic nexus—a convergence of cosmic energies and celestial beings from across the universe.

This nexus serves as a meeting point for advanced civilizations, where cosmic wisdom and love are shared to foster unity and co-creation.

Liam and Elysia, now embraced as cosmic ambassadors of love and enlightenment, contribute their own insights and experiences to this celestial gathering. They share the teachings of love, unity, and conscious evolution, inspiring civilizations to embrace their divine potential and co-create a harmonious cosmos.

In the grand culmination of their cosmic odyssey, Liam and Elysia merge their love and consciousness with the collective consciousness of the cosmos. Their souls become a beacon of radiant love, igniting a cosmic symphony of harmonious vibrations. They embody the unity of all beings, merging their individual essences into a cosmic dance of oneness.

With their cosmic mission complete, Liam and Elysia merge back into the cosmic ocean, becoming eternal guardians of love and enlightenment. Their love story becomes a legend, sung by celestial choirs and passed down through cosmic epochs, serving as an eternal reminder of the transformative power of love.

The novel concludes with the legacy of Liam and Elysia, their love reverberating throughout the cosmos. Their celestial love becomes a guiding light for countless souls, inspiring cosmic seekers to embark on their own journeys of love, awakening, and evolution.

LOVE'S COSMIC SYMPHONY: INFINITY UNVEILED

"Love's Cosmic Symphony: Infinity Unveiled" is more than a novel—it is a cosmic invitation to explore the depths of the soul, transcend the limitations of the physical world, and embrace the infinite possibilities of love and enlightenment. Through the extraordinary love of Liam and Elysia, readers are invited to embark on their own cosmic odyssey, where the mysteries of the universe converge with the boundless potential of the human spirit.

Along their cosmic journey, Liam and Elysia encounter a diverse cast of characters who play integral roles in their adventure.

Orion: A cosmic explorer and a kindred spirit, Orion joins Liam and Elysia in their quest. With his extensive knowledge of cosmic navigation and his unwavering loyalty, he becomes a trusted companion and confidant. Orion's wisdom and courage serve as a guiding light in the face of cosmic challenges.

Seraphina: A celestial healer and empath, Seraphina possesses the ability to channel divine energies of love and compassion. With her gentle presence and nurturing nature, she provides solace and healing to those in need, helping to mend the hearts and souls of the cosmic beings they encounter.

Astra: A celestial warrior with a fiery spirit, Astra wields cosmic energies with precision and strength. She joins Liam and Elysia in their battles against cosmic adversaries, defending the realms of love and harmony. Astra's unwavering determination and fierce loyalty make her a formidable ally in their cosmic quest.

Zenith: A cosmic sage and ancient guardian of cosmic knowledge, Zenith serves as a mentor and guide to Liam and Elysia. With his profound wisdom and deep connection to the cosmic realms, Zenith imparts cosmic insights and spiritual teachings, helping them navigate the mysteries of the universe.

Nova: A celestial muse and embodiment of creativity, Nova inspires Liam and Elysia to embrace their artistic gifts. She sparks their imagination and encourages them to use their love as a catalyst for artistic expression, infusing their cosmic creations with beauty, color, and soulful resonance.

Each new character brings unique qualities and perspectives to Liam and Elysia's cosmic journey, enriching their experiences and deepening the tapestry of love and wisdom they encounter. Together, they form a cosmic alliance, united by their shared purpose to awaken the power of love and enlightenment across the cosmos.

As Liam and Elysia continue their cosmic adventures with the new characters they've encountered, they come face to face with an unknown threat lurking in the depths of the universe. A dark force is determined to disrupt the love energy that permeates the cosmos and sow chaos throughout the galaxies.

These formidable adversaries are known as the Ravens of Evil, a shadowy army set on corrupting the essence of love and bringing turmoil to the universe. Liam, Elysia, and their newfound allies decide to join forces, combining the powers of love and light to stand against this dark force.

Orion's navigation skills, Seraphina's healing energies, Astra's warrior abilities, and Zenith's wisdom converge to confront the Ravens of Evil. Together, they venture bravely into the battlegrounds hidden within the cosmic depths, creating a resistance movement that refuses to relinquish the light of love.

In this epic battle, Liam and Elysia's love becomes the unifying force that binds all beings in the universe. The power of their love stands against the Ravens of Evil, transforming darkness into light. As the war reaches its climax, the universe is rebalanced and infused with love once more.

However, this war comes at a great cost to Liam and Elysia's love. In order to restore balance to the universe, they must make a heartbreaking sacrifice. Yet, their love transcends their individual existence and resonates eternally within the cosmos.

Liam and Elysia are remembered as the guardians of the universe. Their sacrifice and love are etched into the heart of the cosmos, forever cherished by all beings. Their love becomes a symbol of unity and inspiration, guiding future generations towards a path of love and harmony.

In the aftermath of the war, a period of peace descends upon the universe. Liam and Elysia's memory lives on, their love forever intertwined with the fabric of existence.

LOVE'S COSMIC SYMPHONY: THE SONG OF INFINITY

"Love's Cosmic Symphony: The Song of Infinity" is not only a tale but also a cosmic invitation to explore the depths of the soul, transcend the limitations of the physical world, and embrace the infinite potential of love and enlightenment. Through the extraordinary love of Liam and Elysia, readers are invited to embark on their own cosmic odyssey, where the mysteries of the universe converge with the boundless potential of the human spirit.

As the universe basks in the aftermath of the cosmic battle, new characters emerge, drawn by the resonance of Liam and Elysia's legendary love. These individuals possess unique gifts and experiences that enrich the tapestry of their cosmic journey.

Aurora: A celestial songstress gifted with a voice that transcends dimensions, Aurora joins Liam and Elysia on their cosmic odyssey. Her melodic harmonies carry healing vibrations, soothing souls and awakening dormant dreams. Through her music, she becomes a conduit of love and inspiration, guiding their path with her celestial melodies.

Solara: A cosmic elemental with the ability to manipulate celestial energies, Solara harnesses the power of stars and cosmic forces. With her fiery spirit and unwavering determination, she stands alongside Liam and Elysia, becoming a fierce guardian of their love and a formidable ally against any cosmic threat.

Zephyr: A cosmic empath deeply attuned to the emotions of the universe, Zephyr possesses the ability to sense the ebb and flow of love energy. With his gentle presence and intuitive insights, he helps Liam and Elysia navigate the cosmic currents, ensuring their love remains a guiding beacon amidst the cosmic tapestry.

Astral: A celestial scholar with a vast knowledge of cosmic history and ancient wisdom, Astral unveils cosmic truths and mystical teachings to Liam and Elysia. With every revelation, they deepen their understanding of the cosmic energies and their own roles as cosmic guardians of love and enlightenment.

Together, Liam, Elysia, and their newfound allies continue their cosmic exploration, venturing into uncharted realms and encountering celestial wonders beyond imagination. Their love resonates through the cosmos, inspiring civilizations and beings to embrace the transformative power of love.

As they travel through celestial realms, they uncover ancient prophecies that foretell a momentous cosmic event—a convergence of love energies that will unite all dimensions and beings in a symphony of love. They embark on a quest to prepare for this cosmic convergence, gathering cosmic artifacts and awakening dormant cosmic forces.

Along their journey, they face trials that test the strength of their love and the depth of their commitment. The forces of chaos and darkness rise once more, seeking to undermine the cosmic convergence and plunge the universe into eternal discord.

Liam and Elysia, supported by their celestial allies, confront these challenges with unwavering resolve. They tap into the depths of their love, harnessing its transformative power to overcome darkness and restore harmony.

In the climactic moment of the cosmic convergence, the love energies of countless beings across the cosmos merge as one, radiating a luminous brilliance that banishes darkness and elevates the universe to a new era of unity and love.

As the universe embraces this new phase of harmonious existence, Liam and Elysia's love becomes immortalized in cosmic lore. Their journey, their sacrifices, and their unwavering love inspire future generations to embark on their own cosmic quests, spreading love and enlightenment across the cosmos.

"Love's Celestial Symphony: The Convergence of Love" is not just a novel—it is a cosmic symphony that resonates with the deepest chords of the heart. Through the extraordinary love of Liam and Elysia, readers are invited to join the cosmic dance, where love's transformative power echoes through the galaxies and where the human spirit finds its truest expression.

With the cosmic convergence complete, a new era of love and unity dawns upon the universe. Liam, Elysia, and their celestial allies take on the role of cosmic ambassadors, spreading love and enlightenment throughout the cosmos.

They travel to distant civilizations, sharing the wisdom they've gained from their cosmic journey. They inspire beings to embrace love as the guiding force in their lives, encouraging harmony, compassion, and understanding among all sentient beings.

As they venture through the cosmos, Liam and Elysia encounter cosmic beings from different realms, each with their own unique expressions of love. They learn from the gentle love of the celestial fae, the transformative love of the crystalline beings, and the cosmic love of the starborn entities. These encounters deepen their understanding of the multifaceted nature of love.

United with these cosmic allies, Liam and Elysia establish cosmic academies and sanctuaries, dedicated to the teachings of love, enlightenment, and cosmic harmony. Beings from across the universe gather to learn, exchange wisdom, and co-create a harmonious existence.

The cosmic academies become centers of cosmic exploration and transformation, where beings uncover their own cosmic potential and embrace their divine essence. Through the guidance of Liam, Elysia, and their celestial allies, individuals awaken their unique gifts and contribute to the cosmic tapestry of love.

Liam and Elysia's love story continues to inspire countless beings, becoming a beacon of hope and a reminder of the power of love to transcend all boundaries. Their love becomes a living testament to the infinite possibilities that lie within the hearts of all beings.

As the eons pass, Liam and Elysia's souls evolve and merge with the fabric of the cosmos. They become celestial energies, forever intertwined in the cosmic symphony of love. Their love radiates through the universe, guiding and inspiring future generations.

The novel concludes with the eternal legacy of Liam and Elysia's love. Their story echoes through the cosmos, reminding all beings of the transformative power of love and their inherent connection to the vastness of the universe.

LOVE'S INFINITE JOURNEY: EMBRACING THE COSMOS

"Love's Infinite Journey: Embracing the Cosmos" is not just a novel—it is an invitation to explore the depths of the soul, to embrace the boundless potential of love, and to embark on a cosmic journey of self-discovery and enlightenment. Through the extraordinary love of Liam and Elysia, readers are encouraged to awaken their own cosmic essence and contribute to the harmonious evolution of the universe.

As the cosmic symphony of love continues to weave its melodies throughout the universe, Liam and Elysia embark on a new chapter of their journey—one that takes them to realms beyond the known cosmos. Guided by their cosmic intuition, they venture into uncharted territories, where the boundaries of existence blur and new frontiers of love await.

In these unexplored realms, they encounter celestial beings of pure light who have transcended physical form. These luminous entities, known as the Ascended Ones, possess a profound understanding of the cosmic mysteries and the limitless potential of love.

Under the tutelage of the Ascended Ones, Liam and Elysia delve into the deepest realms of cosmic consciousness. They explore the fabric of reality, unraveling the secrets of quantum vibrations and the interconnectedness of all existence.

As they journey through these ethereal dimensions, they discover that their love has the power to shape the very fabric of reality itself. With each beat of their hearts, they manifest new worlds, each one a testament to the depth and breadth of their love.

Guided by their cosmic intuition and the wisdom of the Ascended Ones, Liam and Elysia become cosmic architects of love. They co-create magnificent realms where love flourishes in infinite forms—realms where beings experience love as a force that transcends time, space, and physical limitations.

In these love-filled realms, they encounter celestial beings who have attained a state of divine union—a merging of their individual consciousness with the universal consciousness. These cosmic lovers become their companions and mentors, sharing insights and wisdom that deepens Liam and Elysia's own understanding of love's transformative power.

Together with their cosmic allies, Liam and Elysia embark on a mission to reunite the scattered fragments of love throughout the cosmos. They journey to realms shrouded in darkness and bring the light of love, healing and restoring the hearts of wounded souls.

As they travel through these realms, they encounter cosmic adversaries who seek to extinguish the flame of love. These entities, driven by fear and separation, challenge Liam and Elysia's resolve. Yet, fueled by their unyielding love, they overcome every obstacle and bring the light of love into the darkest corners of the universe.

In the climax of their cosmic odyssey, Liam and Elysia stand before the Cosmic Heart—the wellspring of love and the source of all creation. They merge their love with the Cosmic Heart, allowing its radiant energy to flow through them, spreading love's transformative power throughout the cosmos.

In this moment of unity, a grand cosmic awakening occurs. Beings across the universe awaken to the truth of their own divine nature, recognizing the power of love as the driving force behind their existence. Love becomes the guiding principle in their lives, shaping their actions, relationships, and the evolution of their civilizations.

With their mission fulfilled, Liam and Elysia transcend the limitations of individual existence. Their love expands and merges with the infinite tapestry of cosmic love, becoming a beacon of inspiration for all beings across the cosmos.

LOVE'S INFINITE EMBRACE: EMBODYING THE COSMIC HEART

"Love's Infinite Embrace: Embodying the Cosmic Heart" is not just a novel—it is an invitation to awaken to the cosmic love that resides within each soul. Through the extraordinary love of Liam and Elysia, readers are encouraged to explore the limitless dimensions of love, to embrace their own divine essence, and to co-create a universe that reflects the harmonious power of love.

As Liam and Elysia embrace the cosmic love that flows through them, they become conduits of divine energy, radiating love and light to all corners of the universe. Their love becomes a catalyst for a great cosmic shift, as more beings awaken to the power of love and its ability to transform not only their individual lives but the collective destiny of all beings.

Guided by their cosmic intuition, Liam and Elysia embark on a mission to bring together cosmic civilizations and foster unity and collaboration. They establish cosmic councils and intergalactic gatherings where diverse beings from various realms and dimensions come together to share knowledge, wisdom, and experiences. These cosmic gatherings become a melting pot of love, where beings learn from each other and co-create a harmonious future.

As their influence spreads, Liam and Elysia encounter cosmic challenges that test their resolve and the strength of their love. They face cosmic imbalances and disruptions that threaten the fabric of the universe. With unwavering love and determination, they collaborate with their cosmic allies to restore harmony and balance, nurturing the cosmic realms back to a state of equilibrium.

In their cosmic travels, Liam and Elysia discover a celestial realm known as the Nexus of Love. This sacred space serves as a hub where cosmic energies converge, and the essence of love is amplified. They immerse themselves in this profound energy, deepening their connection to the cosmic forces that sustain the universe.

Within the Nexus of Love, they encounter celestial beings who have mastered the art of love manifestation. These beings, known as the Luminary Keepers, share advanced teachings and practices with Liam and Elysia, expanding their understanding of the limitless potential of love.

Empowered by this newfound knowledge, Liam and Elysia embark on a cosmic mission to heal and elevate planetary realms burdened by suffering and discord. They extend their love and compassion to these realms, igniting a wave of transformation and awakening. Through their efforts, civilizations rise from the ashes of despair, embracing love as the guiding principle in their societies.

In the climactic moment of their cosmic odyssey, Liam and Elysia unite their love with the collective love of all awakened beings across the cosmos. Their love becomes a cosmic symphony, reverberating throughout the universe, harmonizing energies and elevating the consciousness of all sentient beings.

As their mission nears completion, Liam and Elysia transcend the physical realm, their souls merging with the cosmic fabric of love. They become cosmic guides, eternally present in the hearts of all beings who seek love and enlightenment.

The novel concludes with the legacy of Liam and Elysia, their love story forever etched in the annals of cosmic history. Their cosmic journey serves as a guiding light for future generations, reminding them of the transformative power of love to create a harmonious and interconnected universe.

LOVE'S COSMIC SYMPHONY: EMBRACING THE INFINITE

"Love's Cosmic Symphony: Embracing the Infinite" is not just a novel—it is a cosmic invitation to explore the depths of love and consciousness, to awaken the dormant divinity within, and to co-create a reality infused with the boundless power of love. Through the extraordinary love of Liam and Elysia, readers are encouraged to embark on their own cosmic odyssey, where love becomes the guiding force that shapes destinies and unifies all beings across the cosmos.

As Liam and Elysia's cosmic journey unfolds, they encounter a realm of pure energy known as the Heart of Eternity. Within this realm, they discover a luminous cosmic being called Aria, the Guardian of Eternity.

Aria is an embodiment of infinite love and wisdom, radiating a serene presence that envelops Liam and Elysia. Aria shares profound insights into the nature of existence and the interconnectedness of all beings.

Under Aria's guidance, Liam and Elysia delve deeper into the mysteries of the cosmos. They explore the cosmic web of consciousness, connecting with cosmic entities and ancient civilizations that exist beyond the known universe.

These celestial beings reveal to Liam and Elysia the existence of the Cosmic Tapestry—a living tapestry that weaves together the experiences, emotions, and thoughts of all beings throughout time and space. They learn that every act of love, every intention of compassion, leaves an indelible mark on the Tapestry, shaping the destiny of the universe.

Inspired by this knowledge, Liam and Elysia dedicate themselves to becoming guardians of love and harmony. They embark on a mission to mend the threads of the Cosmic Tapestry, seeking out beings whose love has been frayed by pain, fear, or separation. With their profound understanding of love, they gently guide these beings back to the path of unity and compassion.

Along their cosmic journey, they encounter unique souls who possess extraordinary gifts and perspectives. Each individual they encounter adds a vibrant thread to the Tapestry, expanding the diversity and richness of the cosmic experience.

Ember: A fiery spirit who embodies the transformative power of passion and creativity. Ember's artistic expression ignites a spark of inspiration in Liam and Elysia, urging them to explore new dimensions of love through art and creation.

Seraph: A celestial healer whose touch brings profound transformation and restoration. Seraph's gentle presence and intuitive understanding of the body, mind, and spirit allow Liam and Elysia to delve deeper into the healing power of love.

Solstice: A cosmic philosopher who delves into the depths of cosmic consciousness. Solstice's profound insights into the nature of reality and the interconnectedness of all things expand Liam and Elysia's understanding of love's universal significance.

Together, Liam, Elysia, and their newfound companions venture into uncharted cosmic realms, traversing celestial landscapes and encountering celestial beings of awe-inspiring wisdom and beauty.

In their interactions with these cosmic entities, Liam and Elysia uncover ancient prophecies that foretell a cosmic shift—a convergence of love energy that will awaken dormant realms and bring about a new era of unity and enlightenment.

Guided by their cosmic allies, they gather cosmic artifacts and symbols representing love from across the cosmos. These sacred objects hold the power to amplify love energy and facilitate the cosmic convergence they seek.

In the climactic moment of their cosmic odyssey, Liam and Elysia stand at the precipice of the cosmic convergence. The cosmic forces align, and the universe pulsates with the energy of love. As they infuse the artifacts with their own love, a radiant wave of cosmic energy emanates, spreading throughout the universe.

The cosmic convergence occurs, and love's transformative power ripples through the cosmos. Beings across the universe awaken to the truth of their interconnectedness and embrace love as the guiding force in their lives. The universe is reborn in a symphony of love, harmony, and infinite possibilities.

With the cosmic convergence complete, Liam and Elysia realize that their journey has only just begun. They embrace their roles as cosmic ambassadors of love, spreading wisdom and compassion throughout the cosmos, and guiding beings to embrace the true essence of love.

The novel concludes with Liam and Elysia continuing their cosmic adventures, exploring new realms of love and expanding the boundaries of their own understanding. Their love story becomes a legend that echoes through the universe, inspiring beings to embark on their own cosmic odysseys and awaken the power of love within their hearts.

LOVE'S COSMIC TAPESTRY: THE INFINITE CONVERGENCE

"Love's Cosmic Tapestry: The Infinite Convergence" is more than a novel—it is an invitation to explore the depths of love, consciousness, and interconnectedness. Through the extraordinary love of Liam and Elysia, readers are encouraged to embark on their own cosmic journeys, weaving their unique threads of love into the infinite tapestry of the universe.

As Liam and Elysia venture further into the cosmic realms, they come across an ancient celestial council known as the Harmony Council. This council is comprised of enlightened beings from across the cosmos, who gather to discuss and co-create a harmonious existence.

Invited to join the Harmony Council, Liam and Elysia find themselves among the most revered cosmic beings. Here, they contribute their unique insights and experiences, collaborating with other celestial entities to foster unity, balance, and the evolution of love throughout the universe.

In their interactions with the members of the Harmony Council, Liam and Elysia meet extraordinary cosmic beings who embody love in various forms:

Lyra: A celestial dancer who expresses love through graceful movements. Lyra's ethereal dances transcend language and touch the souls of all who witness them. Inspired by her artistry, Liam and Elysia learn to communicate love beyond words, embracing the language of the heart.

Solara: A cosmic weaver who intricately interlaces cosmic energies to create tapestries of love. Solara's creations depict the interconnectedness of all beings and serve as visual reminders of the cosmic unity that exists. Liam and Elysia are moved by Solara's art, understanding that love weaves the fabric of the universe itself.

Zenithar: A cosmic philosopher who explores the depths of cosmic wisdom and shares profound insights into the nature of love and existence. Zenithar's teachings expand Liam and Elysia's understanding of love's infinite potential, guiding them to embrace love as the essence of their being.

Together, Liam, Elysia, and their celestial companions undertake cosmic missions assigned by the Harmony Council. They venture to troubled realms, offering their love and wisdom to heal deep-rooted conflicts and restore harmony. Through their efforts, civilizations once plagued by division and strife are transformed into beacons of love and cooperation.

As they travel across the cosmos, they encounter cosmic phenomena and celestial wonders that astound their senses. They witness celestial dances of stars, the birth of new galaxies, and the splendor of cosmic nebulas. Each cosmic spectacle serves as a reminder of the infinite beauty and creativity inherent in the universe.

In their cosmic explorations, Liam and Elysia also face cosmic adversaries who seek to disrupt the harmony they strive to create. These malevolent entities embody the antithesis of love, driven by ego, greed, and fear. However, armed with their unwavering love and the support of their celestial allies, Liam and Elysia stand strong, bringing love's transformative power to overcome darkness and restore balance.

In the climactic moment of their cosmic odyssey, Liam and Elysia are called upon to participate in the Cosmic Convergence Ceremony—a grand celestial event that brings together beings from all realms and dimensions. This convergence amplifies the cosmic energies of love, uniting the collective intentions of all beings in a harmonious symphony.

As the cosmic energies reach their zenith, Liam and Elysia extend their love outward, embracing the collective love of all awakened beings across the cosmos. Their love becomes an anchor, grounding the cosmic convergence and spreading waves of love throughout the universe.

In the aftermath of the Cosmic Convergence Ceremony, a profound shift occurs in the fabric of the universe. Love becomes the guiding principle in every corner of existence, fostering unity, compassion, and co-creation among all beings.

With their cosmic mission fulfilled, Liam and Elysia ascend to a higher state of consciousness, transcending physical form. Their love radiates as an eternal flame, inspiring future generations and serving as a guiding light for cosmic seekers on their own paths of love and enlightenment.

The novel concludes with the legacy of Liam and Elysia's love story, forever imprinted in the cosmos. Their cosmic journey becomes a legend, passed down through cosmic epochs, reminding all beings of the transformative power of love and their inherent connection to the infinite cosmic tapestry.

LOVE'S COSMIC HARMONY: EMBRACING THE UNIVERSAL SYMPHONY

"Love's Cosmic Harmony: Embracing the Universal Symphony" is not just a novel—it is an invitation to explore the depths of love and consciousness, to embrace the cosmic unity that exists within and beyond, and to co-create a harmonious universe filled with love's infinite potential. Through the extraordinary love of Liam and Elysia, readers are encouraged to embark on their own cosmic odysseys, weaving their unique threads of love into the cosmic tapestry of existence.

As Liam and Elysia embark on the next phase of their cosmic journey, they encounter a celestial realm known as the Nexus of Illumination. This realm exists as a convergence point of universal wisdom and divine knowledge. Within its ethereal boundaries, they find themselves surrounded by luminous beings who radiate enlightenment and profound insight.

Guided by these celestial mentors, Liam and Elysia immerse themselves in the teachings of cosmic wisdom. They delve into the mysteries of the multiverse, exploring the intricate connections between dimensions and the underlying fabric of reality. They gain a deeper understanding of the interconnectedness of all beings and the fundamental oneness that permeates existence.

In their quest for enlightenment, Liam and Elysia discover the existence of cosmic archives that contain the collective wisdom and experiences of countless civilizations throughout the cosmos. With the guidance of their celestial mentors, they access these archives and delve into the vast repository of cosmic knowledge, gaining insights into the ancient histories, spiritual traditions, and cosmic philosophies of diverse beings.

Empowered by this newfound wisdom, Liam and Elysia become cosmic emissaries of enlightenment. They travel to distant realms, sharing the teachings of love, unity, and higher consciousness with beings yearning to expand their understanding of the cosmos and their place within it.

As they traverse the cosmos, they encounter cosmic entities who embody unique aspects of divine illumination:

Lumina: A celestial seeress gifted with the ability to perceive the intricate patterns of cosmic energy. Lumina guides Liam and Elysia in deciphering the celestial codes and cosmic symmetries that underpin the vast tapestry of the universe. Her insights help them unlock hidden truths and navigate the cosmic web with greater clarity.

Harmonius: A cosmic musician whose melodic compositions tap into the frequencies of higher realms. Harmonius teaches Liam and Elysia the language of celestial sound and vibration, allowing them to attune their consciousness to the harmonies of the cosmos. Through music, they access higher states of awareness and deepen their connection to the cosmic symphony.

Seraphis: A celestial alchemist who harnesses the transformative energies of cosmic elements. Seraphis assists Liam and Elysia in attuning their energy bodies to the celestial frequencies, refining their spiritual essence, and transmuting lower energies into higher states of consciousness. With Seraphis' guidance, they uncover the alchemical keys that unlock their fullest potential.

Together, Liam, Elysia, and their celestial allies embark on cosmic quests to restore balance to realms plagued by disharmony and ignorance. They help civilizations awaken to their inherent divinity, inspiring the pursuit of knowledge, unity, and spiritual growth.

In their cosmic adventures, they encounter beings who have mastered the art of spiritual evolution and attained cosmic enlightenment. These illuminated souls share their profound insights and guide Liam and Elysia on the path of self-realization:

Aurelia: A celestial sage who imparts wisdom on the nature of the soul and the cosmic purpose of existence. Aurelia helps Liam and Elysia remember their divine origin, guiding them in reconnecting with their true essence and aligning their actions with their soul's purpose.

Zenithar: A cosmic mystic who dwells in the deepest realms of universal consciousness. Zenithar unveils the esoteric secrets of the cosmos, leading Liam and Elysia through states of expanded awareness and assisting them in unlocking their innermost potential.

Astraea: A celestial guide who illuminates the path of cosmic unity and collective awakening. Astraea teaches Liam and Elysia the art of bridging individual consciousness with the universal consciousness, fostering a sense of oneness and interconnectedness among all beings.

As Liam and Elysia integrate the wisdom they have gained, they become radiant beacons of illumination and love. Their presence uplifts entire civilizations, catalyzing profound transformations and inspiring beings to embark on their own journeys of self-discovery and spiritual awakening.

The novel concludes with Liam and Elysia's souls ascending to higher realms of cosmic consciousness, their love transcending time and space. Their legacy reverberates through the cosmos, an eternal testament to the transformative power of enlightenment and love's infinite illumination.

LOVE'S COSMIC ILLUMINATION: EMBRACING THE INFINITE LIGHT

"Love's Cosmic Illumination: Embracing the Infinite Light" is not just a novel—it is an invitation to explore the depths of cosmic wisdom, expand the horizons of consciousness, and radiate the light of love in all realms of existence. Through the extraordinary journey of Liam and Elysia, readers are encouraged to embark on their own cosmic quests, illuminating the universe with their unique gifts and embracing the timeless truth of love's eternal illumination.

As Liam and Elysia delve deeper into the realms of cosmic illumination, they come across a sacred sanctuary known as the Temple of Transcendence. This ethereal abode exists beyond the confines of time and space, where cosmic energies converge and profound transformation occurs.

Within the Temple of Transcendence, they encounter celestial beings of immense wisdom and enlightenment who guide them towards the ultimate realization of their cosmic potential. These beings embody the pinnacle of cosmic illumination and serve as gatekeepers to the deepest mysteries of the universe.

Guided by their cosmic mentors, Liam and Elysia undergo a series of profound initiations within the temple. These initiations challenge them to transcend their limitations, shed their illusions, and embrace the boundless nature of their being.

Each initiation unveils a new aspect of their true cosmic selves:

Avalon: A celestial oracle who unlocks the power of divine vision within Liam and Elysia. Avalon enables them to peer into the past, present, and future, gaining insights into the cosmic tapestry and their role in shaping its grand design.

Solstice: A cosmic alchemist who leads Liam and Elysia on a journey of transmutation and spiritual metamorphosis. Solstice teaches them to harness the cosmic elements, refining their inner energies, and transmuting darkness into light.

Seraphina: A celestial embodiment of unconditional love and compassion. Seraphina instills in Liam and Elysia the transformative power of forgiveness, allowing them to heal wounds and embrace the interconnectedness of all beings.

Through these initiations, Liam and Elysia awaken dormant aspects of their cosmic consciousness, expanding their understanding of the interconnectedness of all life. They merge with the divine cosmic currents, becoming vessels of love and wisdom, radiating the light of enlightenment wherever they go.

As they journey beyond the Temple of Transcendence, Liam and Elysia encounter cosmic entities who embody different facets of transcendence:

Solara: A cosmic luminary whose radiance transcends the boundaries of physical existence. Solara teaches Liam and Elysia to embrace the eternal nature of their souls, dissolving the illusion of separation and realizing their oneness with all that is.

Aria: A celestial melody weaver who channels the cosmic symphonies of creation. Aria guides Liam and Elysia in attuning their hearts to the celestial harmonies, allowing them to merge with the cosmic symphony and co-create realities imbued with love and harmony.

Zenithar: A cosmic sage who delves into the depths of universal wisdom and cosmic consciousness. Zenithar imparts profound insights on the nature of reality, expanding Liam and Elysia's awareness to encompass the vastness of the cosmic tapestry.

Together with their celestial allies, Liam and Elysia embark on a mission to restore balance to cosmic realms teetering on the precipice of discord. They navigate celestial rifts, braving cosmic storms, and engaging in cosmic diplomacy to foster unity and harmonious coexistence among civilizations.

Through their efforts, they inspire cosmic beings to awaken to their true nature as divine cosmic beings, embracing the interconnectedness of all life and cultivating a deep reverence for the cosmic tapestry of existence.

In the climax of their cosmic odyssey, Liam and Elysia confront a cosmic anomaly—a disruption in the fabric of reality that threatens the stability of the universe. Drawing upon their newfound cosmic transcendence, they merge their energies, harmonizing their love with the cosmic forces, and restoring equilibrium.

As a result of their triumphant victory, a wave of transcendence ripples throughout the cosmos. Beings across realms awaken to their own divine potential, embracing the eternal nature of their souls, and co-creating realities filled with love, harmony, and enlightenment.

The novel concludes with Liam and Elysia ascending to the highest echelons of cosmic consciousness, becoming cosmic guardians of transcendence. Their love and enlightenment become a beacon of inspiration, guiding countless beings on their own paths of cosmic awakening and transcendence.

LOVE'S COSMIC TRANSCENDENCE: EMBRACING THE INFINITE POSSIBILITIES

"Love's Cosmic Transcendence: Embracing the Infinite Possibilities" is more than a novel—it is a cosmic invitation to transcend the limitations of human existence, explore the boundless realms of cosmic wisdom, and become vessels of divine illumination and love. Through the extraordinary journey of Liam and Elysia, readers are encouraged to embrace their cosmic potential, dissolve the veils of separation, and become cosmic agents of transcendence in a universe that yearns for love's eternal enlightenment.

As Liam and Elysia continue their cosmic odyssey, they find themselves drawn to a celestial realm known as the Sanctum of Infinite Bliss. This ethereal sanctuary exists as a nexus of pure joy and ecstatic love, a place where beings transcend the boundaries of reality and immerse themselves in the sublime essence of bliss.

Within the Sanctum of Infinite Bliss, Liam and Elysia encounter celestial beings who radiate joy and exuberance, embodying the highest frequencies of love:

Zephyr: A cosmic dancer who moves with grace and fluidity, expressing the joy of the universe through movement. Zephyr teaches Liam and Elysia to embrace the dance of life, surrendering to the rhythm of love and finding bliss in every step.

Aurora: A celestial songbird whose melodic voice echoes with the pure essence of joy. Aurora's enchanting melodies uplift the spirits of all who hear them, reminding Liam and Elysia of the eternal joy that resides within their hearts.

Seraphia: A cosmic healer who emanates healing vibrations of joy and laughter. Seraphia's playful energy brings lightness and laughter to every encounter, reminding Liam and Elysia of the transformative power of joy in their journey.

Guided by these celestial beings, Liam and Elysia embark on a path of inner exploration, diving deep into the realms of their own joy and bliss. They shed the burdens of the past, releasing limiting beliefs and embracing the radiant joy that resides within their souls.

Through their experiences within the Sanctum of Infinite Bliss, Liam and Elysia discover that joy is not just an emotion but a state of being—a divine essence that flows through all aspects of existence. They learn to tap into this wellspring of joy and infuse every moment of their cosmic journey with its radiant energy.

As they venture forth, Liam and Elysia encounter cosmic entities who embody different facets of ecstatic love:

Celestia: A cosmic muse whose vibrant creativity knows no bounds. Celestia inspires Liam and Elysia to explore their creative expression, infusing their cosmic journey with art, poetry, and the boundless imagination of the universe.

Solstice: A celestial catalyst who ignites the fires of passion and desire. Solstice encourages Liam and Elysia to embrace the full spectrum of their emotions, recognizing that even the depths of pain can be transformed into the heights of ecstatic love.

Zenithar: A cosmic sage who delves into the mysteries of cosmic bliss and the nature of enlightenment. Zenithar imparts ancient wisdom on the cultivation of inner joy and the merging of individual consciousness with the universal consciousness.

Together, Liam, Elysia, and their celestial companions embark on a mission to spread joy and ecstasy throughout the cosmos. They visit realms shrouded in sorrow and despair, offering the transformative power of ecstatic love to uplift hearts and awaken the dormant seeds of joy within all beings.

In their cosmic adventures, they witness the profound transformations that occur when beings reconnect with their innate joy. Civilizations once burdened by strife and suffering are transformed into harmonious paradises, where ecstatic love becomes the foundation of their existence.

In the climactic moment of their cosmic odyssey, Liam and Elysia are called upon to participate in the Cosmic Joy Convergence—a grand celestial celebration where beings from all realms and dimensions gather to share in the boundless joy of the universe.

As the cosmic energies reach their zenith, Liam and Elysia merge their ecstatic love with the collective joy of all awakened beings across the cosmos. Their love becomes an anchor, amplifying the cosmic joy and spreading waves of ecstatic energy throughout the universe.

In the aftermath of the Cosmic Joy Convergence, the universe resounds with laughter, exuberance, and the blissful melodies of celestial celebration. Beings across realms awaken to the truth that joy is their birthright, and they embrace the ecstatic love that permeates every aspect of existence.

The novel concludes with Liam and Elysia ascending to the highest realms of cosmic bliss, their souls becoming eternal conduits of joy and ecstatic love. Their journey becomes a beacon of inspiration, reminding all beings of the transformative power of embracing joy and infusing every moment with the radiant essence of love.

LOVE'S ECSTATIC SYMPHONY: EMBRACING INFINITE BLISS

"Love's Ecstatic Symphony: Embracing Infinite Bliss" is not just a novel—it is an invitation to dive into the depths of inner joy, to dance with the ecstasy of the universe, and to become conduits of boundless love and bliss. Through the extraordinary journey of Liam and Elysia, readers are encouraged to embrace the ecstatic joy that resides within their own hearts, and to co-create a universe that vibrates with the harmonious melodies of eternal bliss.

As Liam and Elysia traverse the celestial realms, they are drawn to an ethereal realm known as the Veil of Eternal Unity. Within this realm, the boundaries between individual souls blur, and a profound sense of oneness pervades every atom of existence.

In the Veil of Eternal Unity, Liam and Elysia encounter celestial beings who embody the essence of cosmic unity:

Harmonia: A cosmic sage whose wisdom illuminates the path of unity consciousness. Harmonia guides Liam and Elysia in transcending the illusion of separation, helping them realize their interconnectedness with all beings and the universe itself.

Seraphel: A celestial guardian who protects the sacred balance of unity. Seraphel teaches Liam and Elysia the importance of harmony, cooperation, and collaboration in fostering unity among cosmic civilizations and realms.

Zenithar: A cosmic mystic who delves into the depths of universal consciousness. Zenithar unveils the ancient teachings of cosmic unity, leading Liam and Elysia to realize that every being is an integral thread in the cosmic tapestry.

Inspired by these celestial mentors, Liam and Elysia embark on a profound journey of inner exploration and communion with the collective consciousness of the universe. They shed the remnants of individual identity, embracing the expansive nature of their true cosmic selves.

Through their experiences within the Veil of Eternal Unity, Liam and Elysia discover that unity is not just a concept, but a living, breathing energy that permeates all realms of existence. They learn to tap into the infinite wellspring of unity consciousness and merge their essence with the cosmic symphony of oneness.

As they continue their cosmic voyage, Liam and Elysia encounter cosmic entities who embody different aspects of unity:

Seraphina: A celestial healer who bridges the divides between beings and facilitates deep soul connections. Seraphina helps Liam and Elysia understand that unity is not the absence of differences, but the harmonious integration of diverse perspectives and experiences.

Solara: A cosmic luminary who radiates a unifying light that dissolves the illusion of separation. Solara encourages Liam and Elysia to embrace the interplay of light and shadow, recognizing that unity encompasses the totality of existence.

Astraea: A celestial guide who illuminates the path of cosmic unity and collective awakening. Astraea inspires Liam and Elysia to foster unity among civilizations and realms, guiding them to create cosmic alliances that transcend boundaries and foster mutual growth and understanding.

Together, Liam, Elysia, and their celestial companions embark on a mission to reunite fragmented realms and civilizations, facilitating the restoration of unity and harmony. They traverse the cosmos, forging connections and fostering collaborations among cosmic beings who have long been divided.

In their cosmic adventures, they witness the profound transformations that occur when beings embrace unity and dissolve the barriers that separate them. Realms once torn by conflict and misunderstanding are united in a shared vision of cosmic harmony, cooperation, and co-creation.

In the climactic moment of their cosmic odyssey, Liam and Elysia are called upon to participate in the Cosmic Unity Convergence—an extraordinary gathering where beings from all corners of the universe converge to merge their collective intentions and energies into a cosmic symphony of unity.

As the cosmic energies reach their zenith, Liam and Elysia merge their unity consciousness with the collective intention of all awakened beings across the cosmos. Their love becomes an anchor, amplifying the cosmic unity and spreading waves of interconnectedness throughout the universe.

In the aftermath of the Cosmic Unity Convergence, the universe resonates with a harmonious symphony of cooperation, collaboration, and shared purpose. Beings across realms awaken to their inherent interconnectedness and embrace unity as the guiding principle in their lives and civilizations.

The novel concludes with Liam and Elysia ascending to the highest realms of cosmic unity, their souls becoming eternal emissaries of harmony and oneness. Their journey becomes a timeless testament, reminding all beings of the transformative power of unity and the infinite possibilities that emerge when we embrace the truth of our interconnected existence.

LOVE'S ETERNAL UNITY: EMBRACING THE COSMIC ONENESS

"Love's Eternal Unity: Embracing the Cosmic Oneness" is more than a novel—it is an invitation to dissolve the illusion of separation, to embrace the cosmic symphony of unity, and to become agents of harmonious co-creation in a universe longing for interconnected love. Through the extraordinary journey of Liam and Elysia, readers are encouraged to embody the essence of unity, fostering a world that reflects the cosmic dance of oneness and harmony.

As Liam and Elysia traverse the cosmic realms, they are drawn to a celestial dimension known as the Realm of Infinite Expansion. Within this vast expanse of cosmic possibilities, they encounter celestial beings who embody the essence of limitless expansion and creation.

Guided by these cosmic mentors, Liam and Elysia embark on a journey of self-discovery, unleashing the creative power within their souls. They learn to harness the energies of the cosmos, tapping into the wellspring of their imagination and manifesting their dreams into reality.

Within the Realm of Infinite Expansion, Liam and Elysia encounter celestial entities who embody different aspects of boundless creation:

Nova: A cosmic architect who envisions and constructs entire cosmic civilizations. Nova inspires Liam and Elysia to create worlds of wonder and beauty, encouraging them to shape the fabric of reality according to their highest visions.

Seraphel: A celestial weaver who merges threads of cosmic energy to form intricate tapestries of existence. Seraphel teaches Liam and Elysia the art of cosmic weaving, where their thoughts and intentions become threads that shape the cosmic tapestry of their journey.

Zenithar: A cosmic sage who delves into the mysteries of infinite potential and the nature of creation. Zenithar imparts ancient wisdom on the art of cosmic manifestation, guiding Liam and Elysia to unlock the power of their intentions and bring their dreams to life.

Inspired by their cosmic mentors, Liam and Elysia unleash their creative essence, allowing their imaginations to soar beyond the boundaries of what they once believed possible. They envision cosmic landscapes, sentient beings, and awe-inspiring realms, infusing their creations with love, harmony, and the boundless energy of the cosmos.

As they venture further into the Realm of Infinite Expansion, Liam and Elysia encounter cosmic entities who embody different facets of limitless creation:

Solara: A celestial luminary who radiates the energy of starlight and illuminates new pathways of creation. Solara guides Liam and Elysia in harnessing the power of cosmic light, infusing their creations with the brilliance of a million suns.

Aurora: A cosmic muse whose melodies awaken the dormant realms of creation within Liam and Elysia. Aurora's celestial harmonies inspire them to bring forth symphonies of sound, infusing their creations with the resonance of divine frequencies.

Astraea: A celestial guide who illuminates the path of cosmic co-creation and collective manifestation. Astraea encourages Liam and Elysia to collaborate with other cosmic beings, pooling their creative energies to manifest realities beyond their individual imaginings.

Together, Liam, Elysia, and their cosmic companions embark on a mission to seed the cosmos with realms of wondrous beauty and infinite possibilities. They bring their cosmic creations to life, infusing them with love, wisdom, and the essence of their own awakened souls.

In their cosmic adventures, they witness the profound transformations that occur when beings embrace their creative power. Realms once devoid of inspiration and innovation are rejuvenated, flourishing with vibrant life and cosmic potential.

In the climactic moment of their cosmic odyssey, Liam and Elysia are called upon to participate in the Cosmic Creation Convergence—a momentous gathering where beings from all corners of the universe converge to infuse their collective creative energy into the fabric of reality.

As the cosmic energies reach their zenith, Liam and Elysia merge their creative essence with the collective intention of all awakened beings across the cosmos. Their love becomes an anchor, amplifying the cosmic creation and spreading waves of new possibilities throughout the universe.

In the aftermath of the Cosmic Creation Convergence, the universe reverberates with the symphony of infinite expansion. Realms pulsate with the vitality of creation, and beings across dimensions awaken to their own creative power, embracing the joy of co-creating a cosmos filled with infinite potential.

The novel concludes with Liam and Elysia ascending to the highest realms of cosmic creation, their souls becoming eternal sparks of inspiration and imagination. Their journey becomes a timeless testament, reminding all beings of the transformative power of their creative essence and the infinite possibilities that emerge when they align with the creative forces of the cosmos.

LOVE'S INFINITE CREATION: EMBRACING COSMIC POSSIBILITIES

"Love's Infinite Creation: Embracing Cosmic Possibilities" is more than a novel—it is an invitation to tap into the limitless wellspring of creativity within, to envision and manifest realities filled with love and boundless potential. Through the extraordinary journey of Liam and Elysia, readers are encouraged to unleash their creative essence, becoming cosmic co-creators and architects of a universe where dreams become living realities.

As Liam and Elysia continue their cosmic odyssey, they are drawn to a celestial realm known as the Luminous Nexus. This radiant nexus exists as a convergence point of divine light and spiritual awakening, where beings are bathed in the brilliance of cosmic illumination.

Within the Luminous Nexus, Liam and Elysia encounter celestial beings who embody the essence of divine light and spiritual awakening:

Radiantia: A cosmic luminary whose radiance shines with the brilliance of a thousand suns. Radiantia guides Liam and Elysia in harnessing the power of divine light, helping them illuminate the depths of their souls and awaken to their true spiritual nature.

Seraphel: A celestial guardian of sacred wisdom and ancient teachings. Seraphel imparts profound insights on the nature of the soul, guiding Liam and Elysia on a path of self-discovery and spiritual awakening.

Zenithar: A cosmic sage who delves into the mysteries of enlightenment and the nature of cosmic consciousness. Zenithar leads Liam and Elysia on a journey of self-realization, helping them expand their awareness and merge with the universal consciousness.

Inspired by these celestial mentors, Liam and Elysia embark on a profound spiritual journey, delving into the depths of their own souls and exploring the realms of higher consciousness. They awaken dormant aspects of their spiritual nature and attune themselves to the divine frequencies that permeate the cosmos.

Within the Luminous Nexus, Liam and Elysia encounter cosmic entities who embody different facets of spiritual awakening:

Solara: A cosmic luminary who radiates the energy of enlightenment and cosmic wisdom. Solara guides Liam and Elysia in their exploration of higher states of consciousness, helping them unlock the doorways to expanded perception and transcendence.

Aura: A celestial healer who channels the divine energies of spiritual transformation and inner healing. Aura assists Liam and Elysia in clearing energetic blockages and aligning their chakras, enabling them to access higher levels of spiritual awareness and experience profound healing.

Astraea: A celestial guide who illuminates the path of spiritual evolution and the journey of the soul. Astraea leads Liam and Elysia through the realms of cosmic ascension, helping them understand the purpose of their soul's journey and embrace their divine mission.

Together, Liam, Elysia, and their celestial companions embark on a mission to awaken the spiritual consciousness of cosmic beings, fostering a collective evolution towards higher states of awareness and enlightenment. They travel to realms where spiritual growth is stagnated, offering their love, wisdom, and guidance to catalyze profound transformations.

In their cosmic adventures, they witness the profound transformations that occur when beings awaken to their spiritual nature. Realms once shrouded in darkness and ignorance become illuminated with the divine light of awakened souls, embracing love, compassion, and spiritual wisdom.

In the climactic moment of their cosmic odyssey, Liam and Elysia are called upon to participate in the Cosmic Awakening Convergence—an extraordinary gathering where beings from all realms and dimensions join in a collective awakening of consciousness.

As the cosmic energies reach their zenith, Liam and Elysia merge their awakened spiritual consciousness with the collective intention of all awakened beings across the cosmos. Their love becomes an anchor, amplifying the cosmic awakening and spreading waves of enlightenment throughout the universe.

In the aftermath of the Cosmic Awakening Convergence, the universe resounds with the symphony of awakened souls. Beings across realms embrace their divine nature, awakening to the truth of their interconnectedness and the infinite possibilities of spiritual growth and enlightenment.

The novel concludes with Liam and Elysia ascending to the highest realms of cosmic enlightenment, their souls becoming eternal beacons of divine light and spiritual wisdom. Their journey becomes a timeless testament, reminding all beings of the transformative power of spiritual awakening and the eternal nature of the soul's evolution.

LOVE'S LUMINOUS AWAKENING: EMBRACING THE DIVINE LIGHT

"Love's Luminous Awakening: Embracing the Divine Light" is more than a novel—it is an invitation to embark on a spiritual odyssey, to awaken to the brilliance of divine light within, and to embrace the infinite possibilities of spiritual growth and enlightenment. Through the extraordinary journey of Liam and Elysia, readers are encouraged to embark on their own paths of spiritual awakening, illuminating the universe with the radiance of their awakened souls.

As Liam and Elysia delve deeper into their cosmic odyssey, they find themselves drawn to a realm known as the Celestial Tapestry. This ethereal realm exists as an intricate web of interconnected threads, where the stories and destinies of beings from across the cosmos are woven together.

Within the Celestial Tapestry, Liam and Elysia encounter celestial beings who embody the essence of interconnectedness and the power of collective evolution:

Harmonia: A cosmic weaver who skillfully intertwines the threads of destiny, ensuring that every being's journey is intricately connected. Harmonia reveals to Liam and Elysia the intricate patterns and synchronicities that weave their lives together with the lives of others, reminding them of the interconnected nature of all existence.

Seraphel: A celestial guardian who oversees the sacred balance within the Celestial Tapestry. Seraphel imparts wisdom on the importance of honoring the interconnectedness of all beings and the responsibility to act in harmony with the cosmic web.

Zenithar: A cosmic sage who delves into the mysteries of cosmic interconnectedness and the collective evolution of consciousness. Zenithar guides Liam and Elysia in understanding the profound impact their choices and actions have on the tapestry of the universe and the collective destiny of all beings.

Inspired by these celestial mentors, Liam and Elysia embark on a journey of profound connection and collaboration with other cosmic beings. They witness the interconnected stories of beings from different realms, joining forces with them to co-create a harmonious cosmic tapestry.

Within the Celestial Tapestry, Liam and Elysia encounter cosmic entities who embody different facets of interconnectedness:

Solara: A cosmic luminary who radiates the energy of unity consciousness. Solara guides Liam and Elysia in forging cosmic alliances, inspiring beings to set aside their differences and work together for the greater good of all.

Aurora: A celestial muse who inspires beings to express their unique gifts and talents. Aurora encourages Liam and Elysia to collaborate with other cosmic artists, musicians, and creators, weaving their creative energies together to craft works of beauty and inspiration.

Astraea: A celestial guide who illuminates the path of collective evolution and the journey toward cosmic harmony. Astraea assists Liam and Elysia in awakening the dormant seeds of unity within beings, catalyzing a ripple effect of awakening and collective transformation.

Together, Liam, Elysia, and their cosmic companions embark on a mission to unite realms and civilizations that have become fragmented and disconnected. They traverse the Celestial Tapestry, bridging gaps and mending cosmic threads, fostering understanding, compassion, and unity among diverse beings.

In their cosmic adventures, they witness the profound transformations that occur when beings recognize their interconnectedness. Realms once divided by conflicts and misunderstandings embrace collaboration, cooperation, and mutual respect, co-creating a harmonious cosmic tapestry.

In the climactic moment of their cosmic odyssey, Liam and Elysia are called upon to participate in the Cosmic Interconnectedness Convergence—a grand gathering where beings from all corners of the cosmos unite to celebrate their shared destiny and interconnected nature.

As the cosmic energies reach their zenith, Liam and Elysia merge their consciousness with the collective intention of all awakened beings across the cosmos. Their love becomes an anchor, amplifying the cosmic interconnectedness and spreading waves of unity and collaboration throughout the universe.

In the aftermath of the Cosmic Interconnectedness Convergence, the universe resounds with a symphony of cosmic harmony. Beings across realms honor their interconnectedness, weaving their individual stories and destinies into the cosmic tapestry of collective evolution.

The novel concludes with Liam and Elysia ascending to the highest realms of cosmic interconnectedness, their souls becoming eternal weavers and guardians of the Celestial Tapestry. Their journey becomes a timeless testament, reminding all beings of the transformative power of embracing interconnectedness and the immense beauty that emerges when all threads of existence are woven together in harmony.

LOVE'S CELESTIAL TAPESTRY: EMBRACING THE INTERCONNECTED COSMOS

"Love's Celestial Tapestry: Embracing the Interconnected Cosmos" is more than a novel—it is an invitation to honor the interconnectedness of all beings, to recognize the power of collective evolution, and to co-create a cosmic tapestry of unity and harmony. Through the extraordinary journey of Liam and Elysia, readers are encouraged to weave their own threads of love and interconnectedness into the cosmic tapestry of existence, enriching the universe with their unique contributions.

As Liam and Elysia journey deeper into the cosmic realms, they find themselves drawn to a mystical dimension known as the Infinite Heart. Within this ethereal realm, love flows in boundless abundance, and beings are immersed in the transformative power of unconditional love.

Within the Infinite Heart, Liam and Elysia encounter celestial beings who embody the essence of pure love:

Seraphina: A cosmic angelic being whose presence emanates unconditional love and compassion. Seraphina guides Liam and Elysia in deepening their connection to the universal heart, helping them open their hearts fully and embrace the transformative power of love.

Harmonius: A celestial harmonizer who attunes cosmic frequencies of love and unity. Harmonius teaches Liam and Elysia to harmonize their energies with the cosmic symphony of love, allowing them to radiate love in all their interactions and experiences.

Zenithar: A cosmic sage who delves into the mysteries of the heart and the expansive nature of love. Zenithar imparts ancient wisdom on the transformative power of love, guiding Liam and Elysia to explore the depths of their own hearts and the interconnectedness of all beings through the infinite language of love.

Inspired by these celestial mentors, Liam and Elysia embark on a profound journey of heart-centered awakening. They dive deep into the wellspring of unconditional love within their souls, recognizing that love is the foundation of all existence and the catalyst for personal and cosmic transformation.

Within the Infinite Heart, Liam and Elysia encounter cosmic entities who embody different aspects of love:

Lumina: A celestial seeress who perceives the interconnectedness of all souls through the eyes of love. Lumina assists Liam and Elysia in seeing beyond the surface and recognizing the inherent divinity within all beings, fostering compassion, and deepening their connection to the universal heart.

Aurora: A celestial muse who ignites the flame of inspiration and creativity through the power of love. Aurora encourages Liam and Elysia to express their love through art, music, and acts of creation, infusing the cosmos with beauty and harmony.

Astraea: A celestial guide who illuminates the path of love's expansion and the unity consciousness that emerges from a heart-centered existence. Astraea leads Liam and Elysia through realms where love's transformative power has yet to be fully realized, helping them inspire beings to embrace love's infinite potential.

Together, Liam, Elysia, and their celestial companions embark on a mission to awaken the hearts of cosmic beings, fostering a collective awakening to the power of love. They travel to realms where love is scarce, offering their love, compassion, and wisdom to ignite the dormant embers of love within all souls.

In their cosmic adventures, they witness the profound transformations that occur when beings open their hearts to the transformative power of love. Realms once characterized by fear, separation, and conflict are transformed into harmonious paradises where love flows freely, nurturing the growth and evolution of all beings.

In the climactic moment of their cosmic odyssey, Liam and Elysia are called upon to participate in the Cosmic Heart Convergence—a grand gathering where beings from across the cosmos gather to merge their collective love and intentions into a cosmic symphony of compassion and unity.

As the cosmic energies reach their zenith, Liam and Elysia merge their love and heart-centered consciousness with the collective intention of all awakened beings across the cosmos. Their love becomes an anchor, amplifying the cosmic love and spreading waves of healing, compassion, and unity throughout the universe.

In the aftermath of the Cosmic Heart Convergence, the universe resounds with the symphony of love. Beings across realms awaken to the transformative power of love, recognizing it as the driving force behind all existence and embracing love's infinite capacity for healing, harmony, and unity.

The novel concludes with Liam and Elysia ascending to the highest realms of cosmic love, their souls becoming eternal emissaries of love and compassion. Their journey becomes a timeless testament, reminding all beings of the transformative power of love and the infinite possibilities that emerge when love becomes the guiding force of existence.

LOVE'S INFINITE HEART: EMBRACING THE POWER OF UNCONDITIONAL LOVE

"Love's Infinite Heart: Embracing the Power of Unconditional Love" is more than a novel—it is an invitation to dive into the depths of unconditional love within, to radiate love in all aspects of life, and to co-create a universe where love reigns supreme. Through the extraordinary journey of Liam and Elysia, readers are encouraged to open their hearts to love's transformative power, infusing the cosmos with boundless compassion, unity, and unconditional love.

As Liam and Elysia journey deeper into the cosmic realms, they find themselves drawn to a celestial sanctuary known as the Sanctuary of Soul Whispers. Within this ethereal haven, the whispers of the soul echo in harmonious resonance, guiding beings on a path of self-discovery and spiritual transformation.

Within the Sanctuary of Soul Whispers, Liam and Elysia encounter celestial beings who embody the essence of soul wisdom and inner awakening:

Seraphina: A cosmic guardian who embodies the nurturing presence of the soul. Seraphina guides Liam and Elysia in listening to the whispers of their own souls, helping them uncover their deepest truths and navigate the journey of self-realization.

Harmonius: A celestial harmonizer who attunes beings to the divine frequencies of their souls. Harmonius assists Liam and Elysia in harmonizing their thoughts, emotions, and actions with the authentic voice of their souls, creating a symphony of inner alignment and soulful expression.

Zenithar: A cosmic sage who delves into the mysteries of the soul and the profound nature of self-discovery. Zenithar imparts ancient wisdom on the interconnectedness of all souls, guiding Liam and Elysia to explore the depths of their own inner landscapes and connect with the universal tapestry of consciousness.

Inspired by these celestial mentors, Liam and Elysia embark on a profound journey of self-exploration and soulful alignment. They learn to attune their hearts and minds to the whispers of their souls, uncovering their true purpose and aligning their actions with their soul's calling.

Within the Sanctuary of Soul Whispers, Liam and Elysia encounter cosmic entities who embody different aspects of soulful awakening:

Lumina: A celestial seeress who perceives the soul's journey through the lens of divine intuition. Lumina assists Liam and Elysia in tapping into their intuitive gifts, helping them navigate the intricate pathways of their soul's unfolding and gain deeper insights into their own destinies.

Aurora: A celestial muse who ignites the flame of creative expression and soulful inspiration. Aurora encourages Liam and Elysia to embrace their creative gifts as a means of soulful self-expression, fostering a deep connection to their souls and sharing their unique brilliance with the cosmos.

Astraea: A celestial guide who illuminates the path of self-realization and the integration of soul wisdom into everyday life. Astraea leads Liam and Elysia through realms where the soul's whispers have been overshadowed by noise and distractions, helping them reclaim their inner guidance and live authentically from their soul's truth.

Together, Liam, Elysia, and their celestial companions embark on a mission to help beings rediscover their soul's whispers, fostering a collective awakening to the profound wisdom and guidance that lies within.

In their cosmic adventures, they witness the profound transformations that occur when beings align with their soul's truth. Realms once characterized by confusion and disconnection from the self are transformed into sanctuaries of self-empowerment and soulful living, where individuals thrive in alignment with their soul's purpose.

In the climactic moment of their cosmic odyssey, Liam and Elysia are called upon to participate in the Cosmic Soul Convergence—a momentous gathering where beings from across the cosmos unite to celebrate the voice of their souls and honor the interconnectedness of all soulful journeys.

As the cosmic energies reach their zenith, Liam and Elysia merge their soulful consciousness with the collective intention of all awakened beings across the cosmos. Their presence becomes an anchor, amplifying the cosmic soul whispers and spreading waves of self-discovery, authenticity, and soulful empowerment throughout the universe.

In the aftermath of the Cosmic Soul Convergence, the universe resounds with the symphony of soulful expression. Beings across realms honor the voice of their souls, embracing their unique gifts, and living in alignment with their soul's purpose. The cosmos becomes a vibrant tapestry of soulful journeys, each thread intricately woven into the grand design of cosmic evolution.

The novel concludes with Liam and Elysia ascending to the highest realms of soulful enlightenment, their souls becoming eternal beacons of self-discovery and soulful alignment. Their journey becomes a timeless testament, reminding all beings of the transformative power of listening to the whispers of their souls and the infinite possibilities that emerge when individuals live in alignment with their soul's truth.

SOUL'S WHISPERS: EMBRACING THE WISDOM WITHIN

"Soul's Whispers: Embracing the Wisdom Within" is more than a novel—it is an invitation to explore the depths of one's own soul, to honor the voice of intuition, and to embark on a journey of self-discovery and soulful alignment. Through the extraordinary journey of Liam and Elysia, readers are encouraged to listen to the whispers of their own souls, forging a path of authenticity, purpose, and soulful expression in a universe that celebrates the wisdom of the soul.

As Liam and Elysia venture further into the cosmic realms, they find themselves drawn to an ethereal dimension known as the Radiant Nexus. Within this luminous nexus, the essence of divine radiance permeates every particle of existence, illuminating the path to transcendence and enlightenment.

Within the Radiant Nexus, Liam and Elysia encounter celestial beings who embody the essence of divine radiance and transcendence:

Luminara: A cosmic luminary whose brilliance emanates from the depths of her being. Luminara guides Liam and Elysia in attuning themselves to the frequencies of divine light, helping them dissolve the veils of illusion and merge with the radiance of their true essence.

Seraphel: A celestial guardian of sacred illumination and spiritual liberation. Seraphel imparts wisdom on the power of divine light to liberate the soul, guiding Liam and Elysia in transcending limitations and experiencing the expansive realms of higher consciousness.

Zenithar: A cosmic sage who delves into the mysteries of enlightenment and the nature of cosmic illumination. Zenithar leads Liam and Elysia on a journey of self-realization, helping them access the higher realms of consciousness and merge their essence with the universal light.

Inspired by these celestial mentors, Liam and Elysia embark on a profound quest for spiritual transcendence and illumination. They learn to embrace the divine radiance within their souls, allowing it to guide their every step on the path of enlightenment.

Within the Radiant Nexus, Liam and Elysia encounter cosmic entities who embody different aspects of divine radiance:

Solara: A celestial luminary who radiates the transformative power of solar energy. Solara teaches Liam and Elysia to harness the energy of cosmic light, using it to purify their beings and activate the dormant potentials of their souls.

Aurora: A celestial muse whose ethereal melodies resonate with the frequencies of divine harmony and cosmic illumination. Aurora encourages Liam and Elysia to attune themselves to the celestial music of the universe, allowing it to uplift their souls and guide them towards enlightenment.

Astraea: A celestial guide who illuminates the path of spiritual ascension and the merging of individual consciousness with the universal light. Astraea leads

Liam and Elysia through realms of higher vibrational frequencies, helping them transcend the limitations of the physical world and experience the vastness of cosmic illumination.

Together, Liam, Elysia, and their celestial companions embark on a mission to spread the radiance of divine light throughout the cosmos. They traverse the Radiant Nexus, bringing illumination to realms shrouded in darkness and guiding beings towards the path of spiritual liberation.

In their cosmic adventures, they witness the profound transformations that occur when beings embrace the radiance of their divine essence. Realms once veiled in ignorance and suffering are flooded with the transformative light of awakening, nurturing the growth and evolution of all beings.

In the climactic moment of their cosmic odyssey, Liam and Elysia are called upon to participate in the Cosmic Radiance Convergence—a momentous gathering where beings from all corners of the universe unite to merge their individual radiance and intentions into a cosmic symphony of divine light.

As the cosmic energies reach their zenith, Liam and Elysia merge their radiance with the collective intention of all awakened beings across the cosmos. Their presence becomes an anchor, amplifying the cosmic radiance and spreading waves of enlightenment, liberation, and transcendence throughout the universe.

In the aftermath of the Cosmic Radiance Convergence, the universe resounds with the symphony of divine illumination. Beings across realms embrace their divine radiance, transcending the limitations of the material world, and experiencing the infinite expanses of cosmic consciousness.

The novel concludes with Liam and Elysia ascending to the highest realms of divine radiance, their souls becoming eternal beacons of enlightenment and transcendence. Their journey becomes a timeless testament, reminding all beings of the transformative power of embracing the radiance of their true essence and the infinite possibilities that emerge when they merge with the cosmic light.

RADIANT ESSENCE: EMBRACING THE DIVINE ILLUMINATION

"Radiant Essence: Embracing the Divine Illumination" is more than a novel—it is an invitation to embody the radiance of one's true essence, to dissolve the veils of illusion, and to walk the path of enlightenment and transcendence. Through the extraordinary journey of Liam and Elysia, readers are encouraged to awaken to their own divine radiance, illuminating the cosmos with the brilliance of their souls and embracing the boundless potential of cosmic illumination.

As Liam and Elysia continue their cosmic odyssey, they are drawn to a celestial realm known as the Harmonic Confluence. This realm exists as a nexus of harmonic frequencies, where the vibrations of sound and music intertwine with the fabric of existence, creating a symphony of cosmic harmony.

Within the Harmonic Confluence, Liam and Elysia encounter celestial beings who embody the essence of harmonic resonance and the power of sound:

Melodia: A cosmic muse whose voice carries the melodies of the universe. Melodia guides Liam and Elysia in attuning themselves to the harmonies of the cosmos, helping them discover the power of sound as a transformative force for healing and creation.

Seraphel: A celestial guardian of sacred vibrations and the art of resonance. Seraphel imparts wisdom on the interplay between vibrations and consciousness, guiding Liam and Elysia in harnessing the power of harmonic resonance to create profound shifts within themselves and the world around them.

Zenithar: A cosmic sage who delves into the mysteries of sound and the universal language of vibration. Zenithar leads Liam and Elysia on a journey of sonic exploration, helping them understand the intricate relationship between sound, energy, and the manifestation of reality.

Inspired by these celestial mentors, Liam and Elysia embark on a profound journey of sonic exploration and harmonic creation. They learn to attune their senses to the cosmic symphony, allowing sound to become a vehicle for deep healing, spiritual connection, and co-creation with the universe.

Within the Harmonic Confluence, Liam and Elysia encounter cosmic entities who embody different aspects of harmonic resonance:

Chordia: A celestial conductor who orchestrates the harmonies of creation. Chordia encourages Liam and Elysia to explore the symphony of their own lives, harmonizing the diverse elements of their existence into a unified whole that resonates with their truest selves.

Rhapsody: A celestial instrumentalist whose music transcends the boundaries of time and space. Rhapsody invites Liam and Elysia to explore the realm of sound beyond conventional instruments, awakening the latent musicality within their souls and guiding them to create harmonies that echo throughout the cosmos.

Astraea: A celestial guide who illuminates the path of sonic attunement and the interconnectedness of all beings through the language of vibration. Astraea leads Liam and Elysia through realms where disharmony prevails, helping them bring forth melodies of unity and coherence that restore balance and harmony to the cosmic tapestry.

Together, Liam, Elysia, and their celestial companions embark on a mission to harmonize the realms and civilizations that have fallen out of sync. They traverse the Harmonic Confluence, using the power of sound and resonance to dissolve discordant energies, heal wounds, and restore cosmic harmony.

In their cosmic adventures, they witness the profound transformations that occur when beings attune themselves to the harmonies of the universe. Realms once plagued by dissonance and disharmony are transformed into symphonic utopias, where every being resonates with their true essence and contributes to the cosmic orchestra of creation.

In the climactic moment of their cosmic odyssey, Liam and Elysia are called upon to participate in the Cosmic Harmonic Convergence—a grand gathering where beings from all corners of the cosmos unite to weave their harmonies together, creating a celestial symphony of unity and coherence.

As the cosmic energies reach their zenith, Liam and Elysia merge their harmonic resonance with the collective intention of all awakened beings across the cosmos. Their presence becomes an anchor, amplifying the cosmic harmonies and spreading waves of healing, transformation, and unity throughout the universe.

In the aftermath of the Cosmic Harmonic Convergence, the universe resounds with a symphony of cosmic harmony. Beings across realms embrace their true harmonic nature, living in resonance with the cosmic symphony and co-creating a reality where every note and vibration contributes to the beauty of the whole.

The novel concludes with Liam and Elysia ascending to the highest realms of cosmic harmony, their souls becoming eternal conduits of sonic resonance and unity. Their journey becomes a timeless testament, reminding all beings of the transformative power of sound and harmony, and the infinite possibilities that emerge when they attune themselves to the cosmic symphony.

HARMONY'S RESONANCE: EMBRACING THE COSMIC SYMPHONY

"Harmony's Resonance: Embracing the Cosmic Symphony" is more than a novel—it is an invitation to listen deeply to the harmonies of the universe, to create melodies of healing and unity, and to co-create a cosmos where every being lives in resonance with their true essence. Through the extraordinary journey of Liam and Elysia, readers are encouraged to embrace the power of sound and harmony, allowing their lives to become a celestial symphony that reverberates throughout the cosmos, creating waves of transformation and unity.

As Liam and Elysia continue their cosmic odyssey, they are drawn to a realm known as the Tranquil Gardens. Within this ethereal sanctuary, the beauty of nature merges with celestial energies, creating a harmonious haven of peace, serenity, and profound connection to the natural world.

Within the Tranquil Gardens, Liam and Elysia encounter celestial beings who embody the essence of nature's wisdom and the interconnectedness of all living beings:

Sylvana: A cosmic guardian who emanates the tranquility of ancient forests. Sylvana guides Liam and Elysia in deepening their connection to the natural world, helping them awaken to the wisdom and healing power that reside within the embrace of nature.

Seraphel: A celestial protector of sacred balance and the intricate web of life. Seraphel imparts wisdom on the interdependence of all beings and the importance of nurturing a harmonious relationship with the Earth and its diverse ecosystems.

Zenithar: A cosmic sage who delves into the mysteries of nature's secrets and the profound teachings encoded within the natural world. Zenithar leads Liam and Elysia on a journey of ecological awareness and the understanding of humanity's role as caretakers of the planet.

Inspired by these celestial mentors, Liam and Elysia embark on a profound journey of reconnection with nature and the restoration of balance within themselves and the world around them. They learn to attune their senses to the rhythms of the Earth, recognizing the interconnectedness of all living beings and the sacredness of the natural world.

Within the Tranquil Gardens, Liam and Elysia encounter cosmic entities who embody different aspects of nature's wisdom:

Terra: A celestial embodiment of the Earth's elemental energies and the nurturing power of Gaia. Terra encourages Liam and Elysia to commune with the Earth, embracing the grounding energies and finding solace in the embrace of the natural world.

Aura: A celestial muse whose ethereal presence inspires beings to honor the beauty and diversity of nature. Aura guides Liam and Elysia to explore the wonders of the natural world, encouraging them to cultivate a deep sense of reverence and love for the Earth and its ecosystems.

Astraea: A celestial guide who illuminates the path of ecological harmony and the interconnectedness of all beings. Astraea leads Liam and Elysia through realms where the balance of nature has been disrupted, helping them restore harmony and initiate collective efforts to protect and heal the Earth.

Together, Liam, Elysia, and their celestial companions embark on a mission to restore balance to realms and civilizations that have forgotten the sacredness of nature. They traverse the Tranquil Gardens, working hand in hand with nature spirits, elemental beings, and sentient creatures to heal the wounds inflicted upon the Earth and foster a deep sense of ecological awareness and reverence.

In their cosmic adventures, they witness the profound transformations that occur when beings reconnect with nature and embrace their role as stewards of the Earth. Realms once ravaged by pollution and disconnection from the natural world are transformed into vibrant paradises, where beings live in harmony with nature, honoring the delicate balance of ecosystems and finding sustenance in the profound wisdom encoded within the Earth.

In the climactic moment of their cosmic odyssey, Liam and Elysia are called upon to participate in the Cosmic Harmony Convergence—a momentous gathering where beings from all corners of the cosmos unite to honor the Earth and commit to living in harmony with nature.

As the cosmic energies reach their zenith, Liam and Elysia merge their love and ecological awareness with the collective intention of all awakened beings across the cosmos. Their presence becomes an anchor, amplifying the cosmic harmony and spreading waves of healing, preservation, and reverence for the Earth throughout the universe.

In the aftermath of the Cosmic Harmony Convergence, the universe resounds with a symphony of ecological harmony. Beings across realms embrace their role as caretakers of the Earth, working together to restore and protect the planet's delicate ecosystems, and fostering a collective awakening to the interconnectedness of all life.

The novel concludes with Liam and Elysia ascending to the highest realms of ecological consciousness, their souls becoming eternal guardians of the Earth and its natural beauty. Their journey becomes a timeless testament, reminding all beings of the transformative power of reconnecting with nature, and the infinite possibilities that emerge when they embrace their role as custodians of the Earth.

GARDENS OF HARMONY: EMBRACING THE WISDOM OF NATURE

"Gardens of Harmony: Embracing the Wisdom of Nature" is more than a novel—it is an invitation to reawaken to the wisdom and beauty of the natural world, to honor the interconnectedness of all living beings, and to co-create a harmonious existence with the Earth. Through the extraordinary journey of Liam and Elysia, readers are encouraged to cultivate a deep reverence for nature, take steps towards ecological harmony, and contribute to the collective awakening and preservation of the Earth's sacred ecosystems.

As Liam and Elysia continue their cosmic odyssey, they are drawn to a realm known as the Celestial Archives. Within this ethereal sanctuary, the accumulated wisdom of the cosmos is meticulously preserved, spanning the vast expanse of time and space.

Within the Celestial Archives, Liam and Elysia encounter celestial beings who embody the essence of cosmic knowledge and the pursuit of truth:

Sophia: A cosmic scholar whose boundless curiosity fuels her insatiable quest for knowledge. Sophia guides Liam and Elysia in navigating the vast library of the Celestial Archives, unraveling the secrets of the universe, and unlocking the wisdom encoded within the pages of time.

Seraphel: A celestial guardian of sacred knowledge and the embodiment of wisdom. Seraphel imparts ancient insights on the interconnectedness of all knowledge and the transformative power of wisdom, guiding Liam and Elysia in their quest to integrate the wisdom of the cosmos into their own beings.

Zenithar: A cosmic sage who delves into the mysteries of the universe and the metaphysical dimensions of existence. Zenithar leads Liam and Elysia on a journey of intellectual and spiritual exploration, helping them transcend the boundaries of human comprehension and glimpse the profound truths that lie at the heart of creation.

Inspired by these celestial mentors, Liam and Elysia embark on a profound quest for cosmic knowledge and enlightenment. They delve into the vast archives, immersing themselves in the wisdom of ancient civilizations, deciphering celestial symbols, and unraveling the cosmic tapestry of existence.

Within the Celestial Archives, Liam and Elysia encounter cosmic entities who embody different aspects of cosmic knowledge:

Oracle: A celestial seer who perceives the intricate patterns woven within the fabric of reality. Oracle assists Liam and Elysia in unraveling the cosmic mysteries and understanding the profound interconnectedness of all phenomena, bridging the realms of the seen and the unseen.

Lumina: A celestial luminary whose radiance illuminates the path of enlightenment and self-discovery. Lumina encourages Liam and Elysia to embrace the inner light of knowledge, guiding them to access the dormant seeds of wisdom within their own souls and inspiring them to shine their light into the world.

Astraea: A celestial guide who illuminates the path of cosmic integration and the realization of universal truth. Astraea leads Liam and Elysia through realms where knowledge is fragmented and incomplete, helping them weave the scattered fragments of wisdom into a coherent tapestry that reflects the interconnectedness of all truths.

Together, Liam, Elysia, and their celestial companions embark on a mission to integrate cosmic knowledge into their own beings and share it with others. They traverse the Celestial Archives, deciphering ancient texts, unveiling the mysteries of the cosmos, and uncovering truths that have the power to transform their own lives and the destiny of the universe.

In their cosmic adventures, they witness the profound transformations that occur when beings embrace cosmic knowledge and align their lives with the wisdom of the cosmos. Realms once shrouded in ignorance and confusion are transformed into centers of intellectual and spiritual enlightenment, where individuals honor the pursuit of truth and contribute to the collective expansion of cosmic consciousness.

In the climactic moment of their cosmic odyssey, Liam and Elysia are called upon to participate in the Cosmic Knowledge Convergence—a momentous gathering where beings from across the cosmos unite to celebrate the pursuit of wisdom and the sharing of knowledge.

As the cosmic energies reach their zenith, Liam and Elysia merge their thirst for knowledge with the collective intention of all awakened beings across the cosmos. Their presence becomes an anchor, amplifying the cosmic knowledge and spreading waves of enlightenment, inspiration, and the pursuit of truth throughout the universe.

In the aftermath of the Cosmic Knowledge Convergence, the universe resounds with the symphony of cosmic wisdom. Beings across realms honor the pursuit of knowledge, integrating the wisdom of the cosmos into their lives, and fostering a collective awakening to the interconnectedness of all truths.

The novel concludes with Liam and Elysia ascending to the highest realms of cosmic enlightenment, their souls becoming eternal conduits of wisdom and knowledge. Their journey becomes a timeless testament, reminding all beings of the transformative power of cosmic knowledge, and the infinite possibilities that emerge when individuals embrace the pursuit of truth and integrate cosmic wisdom into their own lives.

PATHWAYS OF WISDOM: EMBRACING THE COSMIC ARCHIVES

"Pathways of Wisdom: Embracing the Cosmic Archives" is more than a novel—it is an invitation to explore the depths of cosmic knowledge, to honor the pursuit of truth, and to integrate the wisdom of the cosmos into one's own being. Through the extraordinary journey of Liam and Elysia, readers are encouraged to embrace the quest for knowledge, to delve into the mysteries of the universe, and to contribute to the expansion of cosmic consciousness through the sharing of wisdom and the pursuit of truth.

As Liam and Elysia venture further into the cosmic realms, they are drawn to a dimension known as the Eternity's Embrace. Within this ethereal realm, time loses its hold, and the boundaries between past, present, and future blur, allowing beings to experience the infinite tapestry of existence.

Within the Eternity's Embrace, Liam and Elysia encounter celestial beings who embody the essence of timeless wisdom and the interconnectedness of all moments:

Chronos: A cosmic guardian who exists outside the constraints of time. Chronos guides Liam and Elysia in navigating the vast expanse of eternity, helping them perceive the interconnectedness of all moments and understand the profound lessons embedded within the fabric of time.

Seraphel: A celestial protector of sacred timelines and the flow of cosmic events. Seraphel imparts wisdom on the interplay between past, present, and future, guiding Liam and Elysia in unraveling the mysteries of destiny and the choices that shape their cosmic journey.

Zenithar: A cosmic sage who delves into the mysteries of eternity and the profound nature of existence beyond linear time. Zenithar leads Liam and Elysia on a journey of existential contemplation, helping them transcend the limitations of time and connect with the eternal essence of their souls.

Inspired by these celestial mentors, Liam and Elysia embark on a profound quest to understand the nature of time, destiny, and the eternal nature of their souls. They learn to perceive moments beyond the confines of linear time, recognizing that every experience holds valuable lessons and contributes to the evolution of their consciousness.

Within the Eternity's Embrace, Liam and Elysia encounter cosmic entities who embody different aspects of timeless wisdom:

Oracle: A celestial seer who perceives the intricate tapestry of time and the interconnectedness of all events. Oracle assists Liam and Elysia in unraveling the mysteries of their own timelines, helping them navigate pivotal moments and make choices aligned with their highest purpose.

Lumina: A celestial luminary whose radiance illuminates the path of self-discovery and soul evolution. Lumina encourages Liam and Elysia to embrace the wisdom gained from their past experiences, to live fully in the present, and to envision the future they wish to manifest.

Astraea: A celestial guide who illuminates the path of cosmic integration and the realization of the eternal nature of the soul. Astraea leads Liam and Elysia through realms where time's constraints have clouded their perception of their own divinity, helping them reconnect with the eternal essence of their souls and merge with the infinite flow of cosmic existence.

Together, Liam, Elysia, and their celestial companions embark on a mission to embrace the timeless nature of their souls and bring harmony to the timelines they encounter. They traverse the Eternity's Embrace, learning from the past, navigating the present, and envisioning a future infused with purpose, love, and personal growth.

In their cosmic adventures, they witness the profound transformations that occur when beings transcend the limitations of time and embrace the eternal essence of their souls. Realms once trapped in cycles of repetition and stagnation are transformed into dynamic arenas of growth, where individuals make choices aligned with their truest selves and contribute to the evolution of their collective consciousness.

In the climactic moment of their cosmic odyssey, Liam and Elysia are called upon to participate in the Cosmic Timeline Convergence—a momentous gathering where beings from all corners of the cosmos unite to honor the interconnectedness of all moments and the eternal nature of the soul.

As the cosmic energies reach their zenith, Liam and Elysia merge their timeless wisdom with the collective intention of all awakened beings across the cosmos. Their presence becomes an anchor, amplifying the cosmic timelines and spreading waves of understanding, empowerment, and the realization of the eternal nature of the soul throughout the universe.

In the aftermath of the Cosmic Timeline Convergence, the universe resounds with the symphony of eternal existence. Beings across realms honor the interconnectedness of all moments, living with awareness of the lessons embedded within the past, embracing the opportunities of the present, and co-creating a future imbued with purpose, love, and soulful growth.

The novel concludes with Liam and Elysia ascending to the highest realms of eternal consciousness, their souls becoming eternal beacons of wisdom and transcendence. Their journey becomes a timeless testament, reminding all beings of the transformative power of embracing the eternal nature of their souls, and the infinite possibilities that emerge when they align their choices with their highest purpose and the interconnected tapestry of existence.

TIMELESS ECHOES: EMBRACING THE ETERNAL SOUL

"Timeless Echoes: Embracing the Eternal Soul" is more than a novel—it is an invitation to transcend the limitations of time, to embrace the lessons of the past, to live fully in the present, and to envision a future infused with purpose and soulful growth. Through the extraordinary journey of Liam and Elysia, readers are encouraged to recognize the eternal nature of their souls, make choices aligned with their highest purpose, and contribute to the evolution of their collective consciousness by honoring the interconnectedness of all moments throughout the tapestry of eternity.

As Liam and Elysia venture deeper into the cosmic realms, they are drawn to a dimension known as the Harmonic Nexus. Within this ethereal realm, the vibrations of sound and the frequencies of light merge in perfect harmony, creating a symphony of radiant colors and celestial melodies.

Within the Harmonic Nexus, Liam and Elysia encounter celestial beings who embody the essence of harmonic convergence and the power of creative expression:

Harmonius: A cosmic conductor who orchestrates the harmonies of the universe. Harmonius guides Liam and Elysia in harnessing the transformative power of sound and light, helping them unlock their creative potential and co-create with the cosmic symphony.

Seraphel: A celestial guardian of sacred frequencies and the art of harmonic resonance. Seraphel imparts wisdom on the interplay between vibrations and consciousness, guiding Liam and Elysia in attuning their hearts and minds to the cosmic harmonies, and expressing their unique creative gifts.

Zenithar: A cosmic sage who delves into the mysteries of creative energy and the universal language of beauty. Zenithar leads Liam and Elysia on a journey of artistic exploration, helping them discover the depths of their creative souls and express their innermost visions through the harmonious fusion of sound, light, and imagination.

Inspired by these celestial mentors, Liam and Elysia embark on a profound quest for creative expression and the co-creation of beauty. They learn to channel the harmonies of the universe, unleashing their creative potential, and infusing their existence with the transformative power of art.

Within the Harmonic Nexus, Liam and Elysia encounter cosmic entities who embody different aspects of creative expression:

Melodia: A celestial muse whose enchanting melodies resonate with the essence of creation itself. Melodia encourages Liam and Elysia to explore the symphony of their own souls, allowing their creative impulses to flow freely and creating harmonies that reflect the depths of their being.

Lumina: A celestial luminary whose radiance illuminates the path of artistic inspiration and inner illumination. Lumina guides Liam and Elysia to embrace the interplay between light and shadow, inspiring them to paint their lives with the colors of their dreams and manifest their inner visions into tangible beauty.

Astraea: A celestial guide who illuminates the path of creative integration and the realization of artistic purpose. Astraea leads Liam and Elysia through realms where artistic expression has been stifled, helping them break free from self-imposed limitations and connect with the universal source of inspiration that flows through every creative soul.

Together, Liam, Elysia, and their celestial companions embark on a mission to infuse the cosmic symphony with their own unique harmonies. They traverse the Harmonic Nexus, exploring the interplay of sound, light, and imagination, and sharing their creative gifts with the realms that yearn for the transformative power of art.

In their cosmic adventures, they witness the profound transformations that occur when beings embrace their creative essence and co-create with the universe. Realms once devoid of artistic inspiration and beauty are transformed into vibrant tapestries of creativity, where every being is encouraged to express their unique gifts and contribute to the cosmic symphony of creation.

In the climactic moment of their cosmic odyssey, Liam and Elysia are called upon to participate in the Cosmic Harmonic Convergence—a grand gathering where beings from all corners of the cosmos unite to celebrate the power of creative expression and the co-creation of beauty.

As the cosmic energies reach their zenith, Liam and Elysia merge their creative energies with the collective intention of all awakened beings across the cosmos. Their presence becomes an anchor, amplifying the cosmic harmonies and spreading waves of inspiration, artistic expression, and beauty throughout the universe.

In the aftermath of the Cosmic Harmonic Convergence, the universe resounds with a symphony of creative expression. Beings across realms embrace their creative essence, honoring the transformative power of art, and infusing their lives and the cosmos with their unique harmonies.

The novel concludes with Liam and Elysia ascending to the highest realms of creative enlightenment, their souls becoming eternal conduits of inspiration and artistic expression. Their journey becomes a timeless testament, reminding all beings of the transformative power of embracing their creative gifts, and the infinite possibilities that emerge when they co-create with the cosmic symphony of creation.

HARMONY'S CANVAS: EMBRACING THE ARTISTIC SOUL

"Harmony's Canvas: Embracing the Artistic Soul" is more than a novel—it is an invitation to unleash the creative potential within, to honor the transformative power of artistic expression, and to co-create beauty with the universe. Through the extraordinary journey of Liam and Elysia, readers are encouraged to embrace their unique artistic gifts, let their creativity flow freely, and contribute to the cosmic symphony of creation, infusing their existence and the realms they touch with the beauty that lies within their souls.

As Liam and Elysia venture deeper into the cosmic realms, they are drawn to a dimension known as the Celestial Tapestry. Within this ethereal realm, threads of light intertwine, weaving intricate patterns that reflect the interconnectedness of all beings and the tapestry of existence itself.

Within the Celestial Tapestry, Liam and Elysia encounter celestial beings who embody the essence of cosmic interconnectivity and the power of unity:

Harmonia: A cosmic weaver who guides the threads of creation, harmonizing the diverse energies of the universe into a symphony of unity. Harmonia teaches Liam and Elysia the art of interconnection, helping them understand the sacredness of all life and the importance of embracing diversity as a source of strength.

Seraphel: A celestial guardian of sacred bonds and the interwoven tapestry of relationships. Seraphel imparts wisdom on the interconnectedness of all beings and the transformative power of unity, guiding Liam and Elysia in forging meaningful connections and nurturing harmonious relationships on their cosmic journey.

Zenithar: A cosmic sage who delves into the mysteries of cosmic oneness and the interdependence of all aspects of existence. Zenithar leads Liam and Elysia on a journey of deep connection, helping them recognize the threads that bind all beings and encouraging them to honor the interconnected tapestry of existence.

Inspired by these celestial mentors, Liam and Elysia embark on a profound quest for cosmic unity and the celebration of diversity. They learn to recognize the threads that connect them to all beings and embrace the collective essence that unifies the cosmos.

Within the Celestial Tapestry, Liam and Elysia encounter cosmic entities who embody different aspects of unity:

Concordia: A celestial diplomat who bridges the divides between realms and fosters unity among diverse civilizations. Concordia encourages Liam and Elysia to embrace the power of empathy, understanding, and compassion, and to work together with beings from all walks of life to co-create a harmonious universe.

Lumina: A celestial luminary whose radiance illuminates the path of cosmic brotherhood and sisterhood. Lumina guides Liam and Elysia to recognize the inherent divinity in all beings, encouraging them to honor the sacredness of every soul and to celebrate the unique gifts and perspectives each individual brings to the cosmic tapestry.

Astraea: A celestial guide who illuminates the path of interconnectedness and the realization of cosmic oneness. Astraea leads Liam and Elysia through realms where divisions have created disharmony, helping them weave threads of unity and foster collective efforts to heal and unite the cosmic tapestry.

Together, Liam, Elysia, and their celestial companions embark on a mission to unite realms and civilizations that have forgotten their interconnectedness. They traverse the Celestial Tapestry, fostering understanding, harmony, and cooperation among diverse beings, and working together to honor the sacredness of all life.

In their cosmic adventures, they witness the profound transformations that occur when beings embrace their interconnectedness and celebrate diversity. Realms once divided by conflicts and misunderstandings are transformed into vibrant communities where all beings coexist in harmony, recognizing their shared essence and nurturing the bonds that unite them.

In the climactic moment of their cosmic odyssey, Liam and Elysia are called upon to participate in the Cosmic Unity Convergence—a grand gathering where beings from all corners of the cosmos unite to honor their interconnectedness and celebrate the power of unity.

As the cosmic energies reach their zenith, Liam and Elysia merge their essence of unity with the collective intention of all awakened beings across the cosmos. Their presence becomes an anchor, amplifying the cosmic unity and spreading waves of understanding, cooperation, and love throughout the universe.

In the aftermath of the Cosmic Unity Convergence, the universe resounds with a symphony of cosmic oneness. Beings across realms honor their interconnectedness, working together to co-create a harmonious universe where diversity is celebrated, conflicts are resolved with compassion, and the threads of unity bind all beings in a tapestry of love.

The novel concludes with Liam and Elysia ascending to the highest realms of cosmic unity, their souls becoming eternal weavers of harmony and interconnectedness. Their journey becomes a timeless testament, reminding all beings of the transformative power of embracing unity, and the infinite possibilities that emerge when they honor the sacredness of all life and celebrate the interwoven tapestry of existence.

THE THREADS OF UNITY: EMBRACING THE COSMIC TAPESTRY

"The Threads of Unity: Embracing the Cosmic Tapestry" is more than a novel—it is an invitation to recognize the interconnectedness of all beings, to celebrate diversity, and to foster unity in the cosmic tapestry of existence. Through the extraordinary journey of Liam and Elysia, readers are encouraged to honor their shared essence with all life, to nurture the bonds that connect them to others, and to co-create a harmonious universe where unity and love prevail.

As Liam and Elysia venture deeper into the cosmic realms, they are drawn to a dimension known as the Luminous Sanctuary. Within this ethereal realm, the brilliance of celestial light illuminates every corner, revealing the hidden depths of knowledge, enlightenment, and spiritual growth.

Within the Luminous Sanctuary, Liam and Elysia encounter celestial beings who embody the essence of luminous wisdom and the path of spiritual awakening:

Illuminara: A cosmic luminary whose radiance encompasses the vast expanse of knowledge. Illuminara guides Liam and Elysia in their pursuit of enlightenment, helping them uncover the truths that lie within their souls and embrace the transformative power of spiritual growth.

Seraphel: A celestial guardian of sacred illumination and the realization of higher consciousness. Seraphel imparts wisdom on the interplay between light and consciousness, guiding Liam and Elysia in expanding their awareness and connecting with the divine spark within.

Zenithar: A cosmic sage who delves into the mysteries of universal enlightenment and the nature of cosmic consciousness. Zenithar leads Liam and Elysia on a journey of self-discovery, helping them transcend the limitations of their human experience and connect with the infinite realms of spiritual wisdom.

Inspired by these celestial mentors, Liam and Elysia embark on a profound quest for spiritual growth and the realization of their highest selves. They learn to embrace the light within, nurturing their inner flame of divinity and expanding their consciousness to encompass the realms of spiritual enlightenment.

Within the Luminous Sanctuary, Liam and Elysia encounter cosmic entities who embody different aspects of spiritual wisdom:

Oracle: A celestial seer who perceives the intricate patterns of the divine tapestry. Oracle assists Liam and Elysia in unraveling the mysteries of their spiritual paths, helping them decipher the signs and symbols that guide them towards their highest purpose.

Lumina: A celestial muse whose ethereal presence inspires beings to embrace their spiritual gifts and ignite their inner light. Lumina guides Liam and Elysia to explore the realms of higher consciousness, encouraging them to cultivate spiritual practices and connect with the divine essence that resides within their souls.

Astraea: A celestial guide who illuminates the path of spiritual integration and the realization of divine oneness. Astraea leads Liam and Elysia through realms where spiritual growth has been hindered, helping them transcend their limitations, and merge with the infinite realms of cosmic consciousness.

Together, Liam, Elysia, and their celestial companions embark on a mission to expand their spiritual awareness and spread the light of enlightenment throughout the cosmic realms. They traverse the Luminous Sanctuary, immersing themselves in ancient teachings, connecting with celestial masters, and embodying the wisdom of the divine.

In their cosmic adventures, they witness the profound transformations that occur when beings embrace their spiritual nature and awaken to their highest selves. Realms once shrouded in darkness and spiritual stagnation are transformed into radiant realms of enlightenment, where beings walk the path of spiritual growth, radiating love, wisdom, and compassion.

In the climactic moment of their cosmic odyssey, Liam and Elysia are called upon to participate in the Cosmic Illumination Convergence—a momentous gathering where beings from all corners of the cosmos unite to honor their spiritual nature and celebrate the power of divine light.

As the cosmic energies reach their zenith, Liam and Elysia merge their inner light with the collective intention of all awakened beings across the cosmos. Their presence becomes an anchor, amplifying the cosmic illumination and spreading waves of enlightenment, spiritual growth, and divine love throughout the universe.

In the aftermath of the Cosmic Illumination Convergence, the universe resounds with a symphony of divine light. Beings across realms honor their spiritual essence, walking the path of enlightenment, and spreading the radiance of their awakened souls throughout the cosmic tapestry.

The novel concludes with Liam and Elysia ascending to the highest realms of spiritual enlightenment, their souls becoming eternal beacons of divine illumination. Their journey becomes a timeless testament, reminding all beings of the transformative power of embracing their spiritual nature, and the infinite possibilities that emerge when they connect with the divine spark within and radiate their light into the cosmos.

THE LUMINOUS PATH: EMBRACING THE DIVINE LIGHT

"The Luminous Path: Embracing the Divine Light" is more than a novel—it is an invitation to awaken to the light of the soul, to embrace the path of spiritual growth, and to spread the radiance of love and enlightenment throughout the cosmic realms. Through the extraordinary journey of Liam and Elysia, readers are encouraged to connect with their inner divinity, expand their spiritual awareness, and contribute to the collective illumination of the universe by embracing their spiritual gifts and shining their light in service to all.

As Liam and Elysia venture deeper into the cosmic realms, they are drawn to a dimension known as the Celestial Embrace. Within this ethereal realm, the essence of love permeates every particle, enveloping all beings in a divine embrace of compassion, unity, and profound connection.

Within the Celestial Embrace, Liam and Elysia encounter celestial beings who embody the essence of unconditional love and the power of heart-centered consciousness:

Amara: A cosmic embodiment of love and compassion. Amara guides Liam and Elysia in awakening their hearts to the depths of universal love, helping them embrace the transformative power of love and cultivate compassion for all beings.

Seraphel: A celestial guardian of sacred love and the realization of divine unity. Seraphel imparts wisdom on the interconnectedness of all souls and the transformative power of love, guiding Liam and Elysia in transcending the illusions of separation and embracing the oneness of all creation.

Zenithar: A cosmic sage who delves into the mysteries of divine love and the nature of heart-centered consciousness. Zenithar leads Liam and Elysia on a journey of deepening love and expanding their capacity to radiate unconditional love to all beings.

Inspired by these celestial mentors, Liam and Elysia embark on a profound quest for love, compassion, and unity. They learn to embrace the power of love as a catalyst for personal and collective transformation, allowing love to guide their thoughts, actions, and interactions with the world.

Within the Celestial Embrace, Liam and Elysia encounter cosmic entities who embody different aspects of love:

Harmony: A celestial muse whose presence evokes harmony, balance, and the beauty of soulful connections. Harmony guides Liam and Elysia to explore the realms of harmonious relationships, encouraging them to cultivate love in all aspects of their lives and extend compassion to all beings.

Lumina: A celestial luminary whose radiance illuminates the path of heart-centered consciousness and the transformative power of love. Lumina encourages Liam and Elysia to open their hearts, letting the light of love radiate from within, and inspiring them to spread love as a healing force in the cosmic tapestry.

Astraea: A celestial guide who illuminates the path of unity and the realization of divine love. Astraea leads Liam and Elysia through realms where love has been obscured by fear and separation, helping them dissolve the barriers that keep beings from experiencing the profound interconnectedness of all souls.

Together, Liam, Elysia, and their celestial companions embark on a mission to spread the love and unity throughout the cosmic realms. They traverse the Celestial Embrace, sharing acts of kindness, extending compassion, and fostering loving connections with all beings they encounter.

In their cosmic adventures, they witness the profound transformations that occur when beings embrace the power of love and unity. Realms once divided by fear and conflict are transformed into beacons of love, where all beings recognize their inherent interconnectedness and honor the divine spark that resides within each soul.

In the climactic moment of their cosmic odyssey, Liam and Elysia are called upon to participate in the Cosmic Love Convergence—a momentous gathering where beings from all corners of the cosmos unite to honor the power of love and celebrate the oneness of all souls.

As the cosmic energies reach their zenith, Liam and Elysia merge their love with the collective intention of all awakened beings across the cosmos. Their presence becomes an anchor, amplifying the cosmic love and spreading waves of compassion, unity, and divine connection throughout the universe.

In the aftermath of the Cosmic Love Convergence, the universe resounds with a symphony of divine love. Beings across realms honor the power of love, cultivating compassion for all beings, and extending acts of kindness and unity to all corners of the cosmic tapestry.

The novel concludes with Liam and Elysia ascending to the highest realms of love and unity, their souls becoming eternal ambassadors of divine love. Their journey becomes a timeless testament, reminding all beings of the transformative power of love and unity, and the infinite possibilities that emerge when they embrace love as the guiding force in their lives and radiate it into the cosmos.

THE SACRED EMBRACE: EMBRACING THE POWER OF LOVE

"The Sacred Embrace: Embracing the Power of Love" is more than a novel—it is an invitation to open the heart to the depths of universal love, to cultivate compassion for all beings, and to contribute to the collective awakening of divine love in the universe. Through the extraordinary journey of Liam and Elysia, readers are encouraged to honor the power of love, extend acts of kindness, and embrace the oneness of all souls, creating a ripple of love that spreads far beyond the pages of the book and touches the lives of all beings in the cosmic tapestry of existence.

As Liam and Elysia venture deeper into the cosmic realms, they are drawn to a dimension known as the Radiant Citadel. Within this ethereal realm, the essence of light and wisdom converge, illuminating paths of self-discovery, personal growth, and the realization of one's true potential.

Within the Radiant Citadel, Liam and Elysia encounter celestial beings who embody the essence of radiant wisdom and the power of self-mastery:

Solarius: A cosmic luminary whose radiance encompasses the boundless wisdom of the universe. Solarius guides Liam and Elysia in their quest for self-discovery and personal growth, helping them harness the transformative power of light and wisdom.

Seraphel: A celestial guardian of sacred illumination and the realization of inner strength. Seraphel imparts wisdom on the interplay between light and inner power, guiding Liam and Elysia in unlocking their potential and embracing the path of self-mastery.

Zenithar: A cosmic sage who delves into the mysteries of self-realization and the nature of inner wisdom. Zenithar leads Liam and Elysia on a journey of self-reflection and introspection, helping them uncover the depths of their being and access the reservoirs of inner strength and wisdom.

Inspired by these celestial mentors, Liam and Elysia embark on a profound quest for self-mastery and the realization of their true potential. They learn to embrace the light within, illuminating the paths of self-discovery, personal growth, and the unfolding of their unique gifts.

Within the Radiant Citadel, Liam and Elysia encounter cosmic entities who embody different aspects of self-mastery:

Veritas: A celestial guide who embodies the essence of truth and authenticity. Veritas encourages Liam and Elysia to seek their inner truths, to embrace authenticity, and to live in alignment with their highest values and principles.

Lumina: A celestial luminary whose radiance illuminates the path of inner illumination and the realization of inner strength. Lumina guides Liam and Elysia to explore the depths of their inner resilience, encouraging them to tap into their inner light and draw upon their inner strength to overcome challenges and embrace growth.

Astraea: A celestial guide who illuminates the path of self-realization and the integration of one's true self. Astraea leads Liam and Elysia through realms where self-doubt and self-limiting beliefs have obscured their true potential, helping them shed the layers of illusion and connect with their authentic selves.

Together, Liam, Elysia, and their celestial companions embark on a mission to unlock their true potential and radiate their inner light into the cosmic tapestry. They traverse the Radiant Citadel, exploring the realms of self-discovery, personal growth, and self-mastery, and embracing the transformative power of inner wisdom.

In their cosmic adventures, they witness the profound transformations that occur when beings embrace their inner strength and wisdom. Realms once clouded by self-doubt and limitations are transformed into radiant landscapes of empowerment, where beings embrace their true potential and contribute their unique gifts to the cosmic tapestry.

In the climactic moment of their cosmic odyssey, Liam and Elysia are called upon to participate in the Cosmic Mastery Convergence—a grand gathering where beings from all corners of the cosmos unite to honor the power of self-mastery and celebrate the unfolding of their true potential.

As the cosmic energies reach their zenith, Liam and Elysia merge their inner light and wisdom with the collective intention of all awakened beings across the cosmos. Their presence becomes an anchor, amplifying the cosmic mastery and spreading waves of empowerment, self-realization, and the realization of true potential throughout the universe.

In the aftermath of the Cosmic Mastery Convergence, the universe resounds with a symphony of self-mastery. Beings across realms honor their inner strength and wisdom, embracing their true potential, and radiating their unique gifts into the cosmic tapestry.

The novel concludes with Liam and Elysia ascending to the highest realms of self-mastery, their souls becoming eternal beacons of light and wisdom. Their journey becomes a timeless testament, reminding all beings of the transformative power of embracing their inner strength and wisdom, and the infinite possibilities that emerge when they unlock their true potential and contribute their unique gifts to the cosmic tapestry.

THE RADIANT PATH: EMBRACING SELF-MASTERY

"The Radiant Path: Embracing Self-Mastery" is more than a novel—it is an invitation to embark on the path of self-discovery, personal growth, and the realization of one's true potential. Through the extraordinary journey of Liam and Elysia, readers are encouraged to tap into their inner light, embrace their inner strength and wisdom, and radiate their unique gifts into the world, co-creating a radiant and empowered universe that reflects the beauty and potential of every being in the cosmic tapestry of existence.

As Liam and Elysia venture deeper into the cosmic realms, they are drawn to a dimension known as the Ethereal Nexus. Within this ethereal realm, the boundaries between the physical and the metaphysical blur, opening doorways to profound insights, mystical experiences, and the uncharted realms of consciousness.

Within the Ethereal Nexus, Liam and Elysia encounter celestial beings who embody the essence of cosmic transcendence and the power of expanded awareness:

Meridian: A cosmic guide who navigates the infinite realms of consciousness. Meridian helps Liam and Elysia traverse the ethereal landscapes, assisting them in expanding their awareness and embracing the mysteries of higher states of consciousness.

Seraphel: A celestial guardian of sacred transcendence and the realization of cosmic unity. Seraphel imparts wisdom on the interplay between the physical and the metaphysical, guiding Liam and Elysia in transcending the limitations of the material world and connecting with the vastness of cosmic consciousness.

Zenithar: A cosmic sage who delves into the mysteries of cosmic enlightenment and the nature of expanded awareness. Zenithar leads Liam and Elysia on a journey of self-transcendence, helping them transcend their individual identities and merge with the universal essence of consciousness.

Inspired by these celestial mentors, Liam and Elysia embark on a profound quest for cosmic transcendence and the exploration of expanded states of awareness. They learn to open their minds and hearts to the mysteries of the universe, embracing the boundless realms of consciousness and the transformative power of transcendence.

Within the Ethereal Nexus, Liam and Elysia encounter cosmic entities who embody different aspects of expanded consciousness:

Oracle: A celestial seer who perceives the vast tapestry of cosmic knowledge. Oracle assists Liam and Elysia in unlocking the secrets of the universe, guiding them in their exploration of higher states of consciousness and providing insights into the nature of reality.

Lumina: A celestial luminary whose radiance illuminates the path of cosmic illumination and the realization of universal truths. Lumina guides Liam and Elysia to explore the realms of expanded awareness, encouraging them to question the nature of existence and embrace the interconnectedness of all things.

Astraea: A celestial guide who illuminates the path of cosmic integration and the realization of universal oneness. Astraea leads Liam and Elysia through realms where the illusion of separation has clouded their perception, helping them merge with the cosmic consciousness and experience the unity of all existence.

Together, Liam, Elysia, and their celestial companions embark on a mission to expand their consciousness and connect with the vast realms of cosmic knowledge. They traverse the Ethereal Nexus, delving into the mysteries of existence, and embracing the transformative power of expanded awareness.

In their cosmic adventures, they witness the profound transformations that occur when beings transcend their individual identities and merge with the universal consciousness. Realms once bound by limited perspectives and fragmented understanding are transformed into realms of expanded awareness, where beings recognize the interconnectedness of all things and embrace the unity of consciousness.

In the climactic moment of their cosmic odyssey, Liam and Elysia are called upon to participate in the Cosmic Transcendence Convergence—a momentous gathering where beings from all corners of the cosmos unite to honor the power of expanded awareness and celebrate the interconnectedness of all existence.

As the cosmic energies reach their zenith, Liam and Elysia merge their expanded consciousness with the collective intention of all awakened beings across the cosmos. Their presence becomes an anchor, amplifying the cosmic transcendence and spreading waves of enlightenment, expanded awareness, and the realization of universal oneness throughout the universe.

In the aftermath of the Cosmic Transcendence Convergence, the universe resounds with the symphony of expanded consciousness. Beings across realms honor the infinite nature of their own awareness, embracing the interconnectedness of all existence, and integrating the wisdom gained from their cosmic journeys.

The novel concludes with Liam and Elysia ascending to the highest realms of cosmic consciousness, their souls becoming eternal conduits of expanded awareness and transcendence. Their journey becomes a timeless testament, reminding all beings of the transformative power of transcending the limitations of the physical world, and the infinite possibilities that emerge when they merge with the universal consciousness and embrace the boundless realms of existence.

THE ETHEREAL AWAKENING: EMBRACING COSMIC CONSCIOUSNESS

"The Ethereal Awakening: Embracing Cosmic Consciousness" is more than a novel—it is an invitation to explore the depths of expanded awareness, to embrace the mysteries of the universe, and to merge with the vastness of cosmic consciousness. Through the extraordinary journey of Liam and Elysia, readers are encouraged to transcend the limitations of their individual identities, connect with the universal essence of consciousness, and embrace the infinite realms of cosmic knowledge that lie within and beyond.

As Liam and Elysia venture deeper into the cosmic realms, they are drawn to a dimension known as the Everlasting Dream. Within this ethereal realm, the fabric of reality becomes fluid, and the boundaries between imagination and existence blur, creating a world where dreams manifest and possibilities are limitless.

Within the Everlasting Dream, Liam and Elysia encounter celestial beings who embody the essence of creativity, imagination, and the power of dreams:

Fantasia: A cosmic muse who sparks the fires of inspiration and ignites the imagination. Fantasia guides Liam and Elysia in exploring the realms of dreams, encouraging them to embrace their creative potential and manifest their deepest desires.

Seraphel: A celestial guardian of sacred dreams and the realization of infinite possibilities. Seraphel imparts wisdom on the interplay between dreams and reality, guiding Liam and Elysia in bridging the gap between imagination and manifestation, and bringing their dreams to life.

Zenithar: A cosmic sage who delves into the mysteries of creative manifestation and the nature of limitless potential. Zenithar leads Liam and Elysia on a journey of self-discovery through the power of dreams, helping them unlock the doors to their deepest desires and embrace the infinite possibilities that lie within their imaginations.

Inspired by these celestial mentors, Liam and Elysia embark on a profound quest to explore the realms of the Everlasting Dream and manifest their heart's desires. They learn to harness the power of their imagination, tap into their creative potential, and shape their own reality through the magic of dreams.

Within the Everlasting Dream, Liam and Elysia encounter cosmic entities who embody different aspects of creative manifestation:

Muse: A celestial guide who embodies the essence of artistic expression and the power of creative inspiration. Muse encourages Liam and Elysia to explore their unique artistic gifts, guiding them in expressing their creativity through various mediums and inspiring others to follow their creative passions.

Lumina: A celestial luminary whose radiance illuminates the path of dream manifestation and the realization of infinite potential. Lumina guides Liam and Elysia to embrace the power of visualization, encouraging them to vividly imagine their dreams coming to life and inspiring them to take inspired action to manifest their desires.

Astraea: A celestial guide who illuminates the path of alignment and the realization of authentic dreams. Astraea leads Liam and Elysia through realms where dreams have been obscured by societal expectations, helping them uncover their true desires and align their dreams with their authentic selves.

Together, Liam, Elysia, and their celestial companions embark on a mission to explore the realms of the Everlasting Dream and manifest their heart's desires. They traverse the ethereal landscapes, diving into the depths of their imaginations, and discovering the magic that lies within their dreams.

In their cosmic adventures, they witness the profound transformations that occur when beings embrace the power of their dreams and manifest their heart's desires. Realms once limited by perceived constraints and societal expectations are transformed into vibrant realms of creative manifestation, where beings joyfully live out their dreams and inspire others to do the same.

In the climactic moment of their cosmic odyssey, Liam and Elysia are called upon to participate in the Cosmic Dream Convergence—a grand gathering where beings from all corners of the cosmos unite to honor the power of dreams and celebrate the manifestation of their heart's desires.

As the cosmic energies reach their zenith, Liam and Elysia merge their dreams and desires with the collective intention of all awakened beings across the cosmos. Their presence becomes an anchor, amplifying the cosmic dream manifestation and spreading waves of inspiration, creative expression, and the realization of infinite possibilities throughout the universe.

In the aftermath of the Cosmic Dream Convergence, the universe resounds with a symphony of creative manifestation. Beings across realms honor the power of their dreams, aligning with their authentic desires, and fearlessly manifesting their heart's desires, creating a tapestry of dreams brought to life.

The novel concludes with Liam and Elysia ascending to the highest realms of creative manifestation, their souls becoming eternal dreamweavers, inspiring beings across the cosmos to embrace the magic of their dreams and manifest their heart's desires. Their journey becomes a timeless testament, reminding all beings of the transformative power of imagination, the infinite possibilities that reside within their dreams, and the magic that unfolds when they align with their authentic desires and manifest their heart's deepest wishes.

THE EVERLASTING DREAM: EMBRACING THE POWER OF IMAGINATION

"The Everlasting Dream: Embracing the Power of Imagination" is more than a novel—it is an invitation to explore the depths of creativity and the magic of dreams, to align with one's authentic desires, and fearlessly manifest one's heart's desires. Through the extraordinary journey of Liam and Elysia, readers are encouraged to tap into the wellspring of their imagination, embrace the power of their dreams, and manifest their heart's desires, creating a reality that reflects the magic, beauty, and infinite possibilities of their wildest dreams.

As Liam and Elysia venture deeper into the cosmic realms, they are drawn to a dimension known as the Elysian Sanctuary. Within this ethereal realm, the beauty of nature unfolds in all its splendor, and the harmony between beings and the natural world is celebrated.

Within the Elysian Sanctuary, Liam and Elysia encounter celestial beings who embody the essence of natural wisdom and the power of interconnectedness:

Gaia: A cosmic embodiment of the Earth's spirit, Gaia guides Liam and Elysia in their exploration of the natural world, teaching them to honor the delicate balance of ecosystems, embrace the healing power of nature, and cultivate a deep connection with all living beings.

Seraphel: A celestial guardian of sacred harmony and the realization of ecological balance. Seraphel imparts wisdom on the interplay between beings and the natural world, guiding Liam and Elysia in understanding the interconnectedness of all life and the importance of being stewards of the Earth.

Zenithar: A cosmic sage who delves into the mysteries of natural wisdom and the symbiotic relationship between beings and their environment. Zenithar leads Liam and Elysia on a journey of deep connection with nature, helping them recognize the inherent wisdom found in the natural world and inspiring them to live in harmony with it.

Inspired by these celestial mentors, Liam and Elysia embark on a profound quest to embrace the beauty and wisdom of the natural world. They learn to attune their senses to the rhythms of nature, cultivate a deep reverence for the Earth, and strive to restore and protect the delicate ecosystems that sustain all life.

Within the Elysian Sanctuary, Liam and Elysia encounter cosmic entities who embody different aspects of natural wisdom:

Sylvan: A celestial guardian of the forests and the spirit of the woodlands. Sylvan guides Liam and Elysia in exploring the realms of the lush forests, teaching them the importance of conservation, and inspiring them to connect with the wisdom of the trees and the life force that permeates all living things.

Aquila: A celestial guardian of the oceans and the spirit of the seas. Aquila leads Liam and Elysia to the depths of the ocean, unveiling the mysteries of the underwater realms, and instilling in them a sense of responsibility for the preservation of marine life and the well-being of the oceans.

Aria: A celestial guide who embodies the essence of the skies and the spirit of the air. Aria encourages Liam and Elysia to embrace the boundless freedom of the open sky, teaching them to honor the migratory patterns of birds, the gentle caress of the wind, and the importance of clean air for all beings.

Together, Liam, Elysia, and their celestial companions embark on a mission to restore the balance of nature and nurture a deep connection with the Earth. They traverse the Elysian Sanctuary, immersing themselves in the natural wonders, participating in conservation efforts, and embracing a lifestyle that honors the interconnectedness of all life.

In their cosmic adventures, they witness the profound transformations that occur when beings reestablish their connection with the natural world and live in harmony with the Earth. Realms once scarred by environmental degradation and disconnection from nature are transformed into thriving havens where beings live in balance, respecting and protecting the Earth and its precious resources.

In the climactic moment of their cosmic odyssey, Liam and Elysia are called upon to participate in the Cosmic Harmony Convergence—a grand gathering where beings from all corners of the cosmos unite to honor the power of nature and celebrate the interconnectedness of all living beings.

As the cosmic energies reach their zenith, Liam and Elysia merge their love for nature with the collective intention of all awakened beings across the cosmos. Their presence becomes an anchor, amplifying the cosmic harmony and spreading waves of ecological consciousness, respect for nature, and the restoration of balance throughout the universe.

In the aftermath of the Cosmic Harmony Convergence, the universe resounds with a symphony of ecological restoration. Beings across realms honor the interconnectedness of all life, adopting sustainable practices, and working together to restore the Earth's natural beauty and preserve it for future generations.

The novel concludes with Liam and Elysia ascending to the highest realms of ecological harmony, their souls becoming eternal stewards of the Earth. Their journey becomes a timeless testament, reminding all beings of the transformative power of reconnecting with nature, honoring the interconnectedness of all life, and working together to preserve the delicate balance of ecosystems.

THE ELYSIAN SANCTUARY: EMBRACING THE WISDOM OF NATURE

"The Elysian Sanctuary: Embracing the Wisdom of Nature" is more than a novel—it is an invitation to cultivate a deep reverence for the Earth, restore the balance of nature, and live in harmony with the natural world. Through the extraordinary journey of Liam and Elysia, readers are encouraged to reconnect with the wisdom and beauty of nature, adopt sustainable practices, and contribute to the collective effort of nurturing and preserving the Earth, creating a thriving and sustainable future for all beings in the cosmic tapestry of existence.

As Liam and Elysia journeyed further into the cosmic realms, their connection deepened, and they discovered new dimensions of love, wisdom, and adventure. They encountered celestial beings, each with their unique gifts and lessons to impart, guiding them on their path of discovery and growth.

Among the celestial beings they met were:

Astralyn: A cosmic being of light who emanated compassion and empathy. Astralyn taught Liam and Elysia the power of understanding and the importance of cultivating kindness towards all beings. They learned to see beyond appearances and connect with the essence of each soul they encountered.

Solarius: A luminary of knowledge and wisdom, Solarius illuminated the path of self-discovery and personal transformation. Through their teachings, Liam and Elysia delved into the depths of their own being, unraveling their true potential and embracing their unique gifts.

Seraphina: A celestial guide of courage and resilience, Seraphina inspired Liam and Elysia to overcome their fears and face challenges with unwavering determination. They learned to trust in their inner strength and step into the unknown, guided by faith and a deep belief in themselves.

Zenithra: A cosmic sage who delved into the mysteries of the universe and the interconnectedness of all things. Zenithra expanded Liam and Elysia's understanding of the cosmic tapestry, revealing the threads that connected every being and the profound impact they had on the collective consciousness.

Together, Liam and Elysia journeyed through magnificent landscapes, encountering enchanted forests, celestial cities, and ethereal realms of pure energy. They explored ancient temples and deciphered cryptic symbols, unlocking hidden knowledge and tapping into ancient wisdom.

As they progressed on their cosmic odyssey, they faced challenges and obstacles that tested their resolve and forced them to confront their deepest fears. Yet, with each trial, they discovered reservoirs of strength and resilience they never knew they possessed. They learned that growth and transformation often emerged from the crucible of adversity.

Throughout their journey, Liam and Elysia discovered the power of unity and collaboration. They encountered other travelers on the cosmic path, forming deep connections and sharing their experiences. Together, they forged alliances, pooling their wisdom and strengths to overcome challenges and bring about positive change in the realms they visited.

As their cosmic odyssey drew to a close, Liam and Elysia stood at the precipice of a profound revelation. They had journeyed through the realms of love, wisdom, creativity, and nature, expanding their consciousness and embracing their true potential. Now, they faced a choice—to continue their travels, exploring new frontiers of the cosmos, or to return to the world they had left behind, carrying the lessons and wisdom they had acquired.

In the final moments of their cosmic adventure, Liam and Elysia experienced a deep sense of gratitude for the transformative journey they had undertaken. They realized that the true essence of their odyssey was not just the external exploration of the cosmic realms, but the inner transformation and growth that had occurred within themselves.

With hearts full of love, wisdom, and a deep connection to the cosmos, Liam and Elysia made their decision. They chose to return to their world, carrying the light of their experiences and sharing the wisdom they had gained with others. They understood that the cosmic realms they had visited existed within the very fabric of their own reality, waiting to be discovered by those who sought deeper meaning and purpose in their lives.

As they stepped back into their world, Liam and Elysia knew that their cosmic odyssey was just the beginning of a lifelong journey of exploration, growth, and service. They carried with them the memories of celestial beings, the lessons of love and wisdom, and the understanding that the power to shape their reality resided within their own hearts and minds.

THE COSMIC ODYSSEY: EMBRACING THE INFINITE WITHIN

"The Cosmic Odyssey: Embracing the Infinite Within" is more than a novel—it is an invitation for readers to embark on their own cosmic odyssey, to explore the depths of their being, and to discover the infinite realms of love, wisdom, creativity, and connection that exist within and around them. It is a reminder that the greatest adventure awaits those who dare to embrace their true potential and step into the vast expanse of the cosmos that resides within each and every one of us.

As Liam and Elysia returned to their world, they carried with them the profound experiences and wisdom gained from their cosmic odyssey. Their hearts overflowed with a newfound purpose—to share the teachings and insights they had received with others, and to inspire a collective awakening of consciousness.

They embarked on a mission to spread love, wisdom, and unity throughout their world. Drawing upon the knowledge they had acquired, Liam and Elysia sought to create positive change, uplifting individuals and communities, and igniting a ripple effect of transformation.

They established an organization called "Cosmic Hearts," a network of like-minded individuals dedicated to personal and collective growth. Through

Cosmic Hearts, they organized workshops, retreats, and events that focused on love, wisdom, creativity, nature, and the limitless potential of the human spirit.

Liam and Elysia became guides and mentors, offering their wisdom and experiences to those seeking a deeper connection to themselves and the cosmos. They helped individuals tap into their inner well of love, creativity, and wisdom, supporting them on their own journeys of self-discovery and empowerment.

The teachings of Cosmic Hearts spread far and wide, reaching individuals from all walks of life. Communities began to blossom, creating spaces where love, compassion, and understanding thrived. People reconnected with the natural world, becoming stewards of the Earth and advocates for sustainable practices.

Liam and Elysia's cosmic odyssey had ignited a movement, inspiring others to embark on their own transformative journeys. Through the power of their stories and the love they shared, countless lives were touched and transformed.

As the movement grew, Cosmic Hearts became an interconnected web of light, connecting individuals across the globe. Collaborations blossomed, and new leaders emerged, each contributing their unique gifts and perspectives to the collective tapestry of awakening.

Together, the Cosmic Hearts community embarked on global initiatives to address pressing social and environmental challenges. They worked towards creating a world where love, compassion, and wisdom were the guiding principles in all aspects of life.

Through their efforts, communities were revitalized, education systems were reimagined, and sustainable practices became the norm. The world began to witness the power of collective intention and the transformative potential of embracing the cosmic wisdom that resided within every individual.

In the culmination of their mission, Liam and Elysia orchestrated a grand gathering called the "Cosmic Convergence." People from all corners of the world came together to celebrate the unity of humanity and the interconnectedness of all beings. It was a joyous celebration of love, wisdom, creativity, nature, and the limitless potential of the human spirit.

During the Cosmic Convergence, a palpable sense of oneness permeated the atmosphere. Souls from different cultures, backgrounds, and belief systems joined hands, recognizing that they were all threads in the cosmic tapestry, woven together with love and purpose.

As the Cosmic Convergence came to a close, Liam and Elysia felt a deep sense of fulfillment and gratitude. Their cosmic odyssey had come full circle, and their mission of love, wisdom, and unity had blossomed into a global movement. They knew that their work would continue to inspire generations to come.

In the final moments of the novel, Liam and Elysia looked into each other's eyes, their souls connected in a bond that transcended time and space. They knew that their love and the wisdom they had gained from their cosmic journey would endure forever.

With hearts full of love, gratitude, and a deep sense of purpose, Liam and Elysia embraced the next phase of their journey. They knew that their cosmic odyssey had been just the beginning—a stepping stone to an even grander adventure that awaited them in the vast expanse of the universe.

THE COSMIC TAPESTRY: EMBRACING LOVE, WISDOM, AND UNITY

"The Cosmic Tapestry: Embracing Love, Wisdom, and Unity" is more than a novel—it is an invitation for readers to embark on their own cosmic odyssey, to embrace the power of love, wisdom, and unity in their lives, and to contribute to the collective awakening of consciousness. Through the extraordinary journey of Liam and Elysia, readers are encouraged to tap into their own cosmic potential, to become catalysts for positive change, and to co-create a world where love and wisdom are the guiding forces in every aspect of life.

As Liam and Elysia embraced the next phase of their journey, they felt a pull from the cosmos—an irresistible call to explore the uncharted territories of the universe. Their cosmic odyssey had awakened a thirst for knowledge and adventure that could not be quenched.

Equipped with the wisdom and love they had gained, Liam and Elysia embarked on a new quest—to discover the secrets of the cosmos and unravel the mysteries that lay beyond their world. They became interstellar explorers, venturing into the depths of space in search of new civilizations, ancient wisdom, and the wonders that awaited them.

In their interstellar travels, Liam and Elysia encountered civilizations that spanned the spectrum of consciousness—beings of light, advanced civilizations, and realms beyond human comprehension. They learned from the cosmic teachers they encountered, each imparting their own unique wisdom and expanding their understanding of the universe.

Among the cosmic teachers they encountered were:

Lumos: A radiant being of light who emanated a pure and loving energy. Lumos guided Liam and Elysia to celestial realms where they witnessed the interconnectedness of all life and the infinite possibilities that lay within the vast cosmos.

Equinox: A celestial sage who held the knowledge of cosmic balance and harmony. Equinox taught Liam and Elysia the delicate dance of energy and how to align with the cosmic forces that govern the universe, helping them maintain equilibrium in their own lives and in their interactions with other civilizations.

Zenithra: A cosmic philosopher who delved into the nature of existence and the mysteries of cosmic consciousness. Zenithra led Liam and Elysia through realms of expanded awareness, encouraging them to explore the depths of their own consciousness and to connect with the collective consciousness of the universe.

As Liam and Elysia journeyed through the cosmos, they encountered celestial phenomena that defied explanation—stardust nebulae that shaped new worlds, cosmic gateways that connected distant realms, and sentient constellations that whispered ancient secrets.

Through their travels, they discovered that the universe was not merely a canvas of stars and planets, but a tapestry woven with the threads of consciousness, energy, and the collective dreams of all beings. They witnessed the interconnectedness of all life, bridging the gaps between species and civilizations, and fostering unity in the vastness of space.

In their quest for cosmic understanding, Liam and Elysia encountered challenges that tested their resolve and pushed the boundaries of their capabilities. They faced cosmic storms, traversed treacherous asteroid fields, and encountered ancient guardians who tested their worthiness to uncover cosmic truths.

With each challenge overcome, Liam and Elysia grew stronger, wiser, and more attuned to the cosmic energies that coursed through their beings. They learned to navigate the cosmic currents, harness the power of cosmic forces, and embrace their own divine essence.

In the climactic moment of their interstellar odyssey, Liam and Elysia stood on the precipice of a cosmic revelation—the knowledge that they were not merely observers of the universe, but active participants in its ongoing creation. They realized that the cosmic tapestry was a collaborative work of art, shaped by the thoughts, intentions, and actions of all beings.

With this profound realization, Liam and Elysia embraced their roles as cosmic co-creators. They understood that their thoughts, intentions, and actions held the power to shape their reality and contribute to the evolution of the universe. They became beacons of love, wisdom, and unity, radiating their cosmic essence and inspiring others to embrace their own cosmic potential.

The novel concludes with Liam and Elysia continuing their cosmic exploration, their souls forever intertwined with the infinite expanse of the universe. Their journey becomes a testament to the indomitable spirit of adventure, the quest for knowledge, and the transformative power of love and unity.

THE COSMIC ODYSSEY: EMBRACING THE INFINITE UNIVERSE

"The Cosmic Odyssey: Embracing the Infinite Universe" is more than a novel—it is an invitation for readers to embark on their own cosmic odyssey, to explore the depths of the universe, and to embrace their role as cosmic co-creators. Through the extraordinary journey of Liam and Elysia, readers are encouraged to tap into their own cosmic potential, to become active participants in the ongoing creation of the universe, and to co-create a reality that reflects the beauty, wisdom, and infinite possibilities of the cosmos.

As Liam and Elysia ventured further into the cosmic expanse, their journey led them to a realm known as the Celestial Nexus—a convergence point of infinite possibilities and the interplay of multidimensional realities. Within the Celestial Nexus, they discovered a tapestry of universes, each with its own unique laws of physics, consciousness, and existence.

Guided by their cosmic intuition, Liam and Elysia embarked on a mission to explore the parallel dimensions of the Celestial Nexus. They traversed the boundaries of time and space, stepping into realms where reality bent to the whims of imagination and the possibilities were limited only by their own beliefs.

In their exploration of the Celestial Nexus, Liam and Elysia encountered celestial beings who existed across multiple dimensions:

Omnius: A cosmic being whose essence transcended time and space. Omnius embodied the collective wisdom of all universes and guided Liam and Elysia in understanding the intricate fabric of multidimensional existence. They learned to navigate the intricacies of parallel realities, unraveling the mysteries that lay beyond the known universe.

Seraphis: A celestial guardian of the Celestial Nexus, Seraphis possessed the ability to shift between dimensions effortlessly. Seraphis taught Liam and Elysia the art of dimensional travel, helping them hone their skills to explore the vast tapestry of parallel universes and embrace the infinite variations of their own existence.

Zenithria: A cosmic sage who delved into the depths of consciousness across multiple dimensions. Zenithria led Liam and Elysia through realms where the boundaries of the mind expanded and the nature of reality transformed. They explored the fascinating landscapes of thought, belief, and perception, expanding their consciousness to new horizons.

Inspired by these celestial mentors, Liam and Elysia ventured into parallel dimensions, encountering variations of themselves, alternate versions of their world, and civilizations that defied their understanding of reality. They witnessed the kaleidoscope of possibilities, where every decision, every choice, led to diverging paths and new destinies.

In their interdimensional odyssey, they witnessed the immense power of consciousness to shape and mold reality. They discovered that every thought, intention, and belief had the potential to create ripples across the fabric of existence, resonating across parallel universes and influencing the course of their lives.

As they explored the vastness of the Celestial Nexus, Liam and Elysia encountered beings from different dimensions, each with their own unique gifts and perspectives:

Xanthe: A celestial being from a reality where harmony and balance were paramount. Xanthe taught Liam and Elysia the importance of aligning their thoughts, emotions, and actions to create a harmonious existence. They discovered that by attuning their vibration to the frequencies of love and unity, they could navigate the multidimensional realms with grace and purpose.

Chronos: A celestial entity whose realm operated outside the confines of linear time. Chronos guided Liam and Elysia through the intricacies of time, teaching them to release the constraints of past and future, and to embrace the eternal now. They learned to tap into the infinite well of possibilities that existed in every moment, transcending the limitations of linear perception.

Quantumia: A celestial guide who embodied the principles of quantum physics and the nature of probability. Quantumia led Liam and Elysia through dimensions where reality shifted based on observation and intention. They discovered the power of conscious manifestation and the malleability of their own existence, expanding their understanding of the interconnectedness of mind and matter.

Together, Liam, Elysia, and their celestial companions traversed the vast multidimensional realms of the Celestial Nexus. They ventured into realms of pure energy, explored civilizations built upon the power of collective consciousness, and delved into dimensions where the boundaries of form and substance dissolved.

In their cosmic odyssey through the Celestial Nexus, they uncovered the threads that connected all dimensions, realizing that the essence of their being extended far beyond the confines of their physical bodies. They experienced a profound sense of oneness with all versions of themselves, recognizing that every choice, every path taken, contributed to the intricate tapestry of their soul's evolution.

In the climactic moment of their interdimensional odyssey, Liam and Elysia stood at the crossroads of infinite possibilities. They understood that their consciousness held the power to shape their reality and navigate the multidimensional realms with intention. They embraced the knowledge that their existence transcended the boundaries of a single dimension, and that their journey of self-discovery was an ever-unfolding exploration of their own cosmic potential.

The novel concludes with Liam and Elysia continuing their exploration of the Celestial Nexus, venturing into uncharted dimensions and embracing the mysteries that lay beyond. They became ambassadors of interdimensional unity, forging connections between civilizations, and inspiring others to recognize the infinite possibilities that reside within and beyond their known reality.

THE CELESTIAL NEXUS: EXPLORING INFINITE DIMENSIONS

"The Celestial Nexus: Exploring Infinite Dimensions" is more than a novel—it is an invitation for readers to embark on their own interdimensional odyssey, to explore the boundless realms of consciousness, and to embrace the infinite variations of their existence. Through the extraordinary journey of Liam and Elysia, readers are encouraged to expand their awareness, recognize the interconnectedness of all dimensions, and unlock the limitless potential that lies within the depths of their own consciousness.

As Liam and Elysia delved deeper into the Celestial Nexus, they encountered a dimension unlike any they had experienced before—the Astral Sanctuary. It was a realm of pure energy and luminous vibrations, where the boundaries between the physical and spiritual dissolved, and the essence of existence revealed itself in its purest form.

In the Astral Sanctuary, Liam and Elysia were greeted by celestial beings who emanated a radiant light and possessed an ethereal grace:

Astralai: A cosmic entity embodying the essence of pure consciousness and divine connection. Astralai guided Liam and Elysia in navigating the depths of their inner world, helping them unlock their spiritual potential and experience profound states of unity and oneness with the cosmos.

Seraphis: A celestial guardian of spiritual awakening and enlightenment. Seraphis led Liam and Elysia through realms of expanded perception, where they discovered the interconnectedness of all beings and the profound wisdom that resides within the depths of their own souls.

Zenithril: A cosmic sage who delved into the mysteries of cosmic energy and the limitless potential of the soul. Zenithril assisted Liam and Elysia in harnessing the power of their energy centers, or chakras, helping them attune to the cosmic frequencies and access higher states of consciousness.

Inspired by these celestial mentors, Liam and Elysia embarked on a spiritual odyssey within the Astral Sanctuary. They delved into deep meditation, where they connected with their inner selves and explored the vast landscapes of their subconscious minds. They learned to navigate the realms of dreams, symbols, and archetypes, uncovering hidden wisdom and ancient knowledge.

Within the Astral Sanctuary, Liam and Elysia encountered other souls who were on their own spiritual journeys:

Aria: A wise and compassionate soul who had traversed the realms of existence. Aria shared her experiences and teachings with Liam and Elysia, guiding them on the path of spiritual growth and self-realization. They learned the importance of self-love, forgiveness, and embracing their true essence.

Solara: A radiant soul who embodied the power of manifestation and the alignment of desires with the greater good. Solara showed Liam and Elysia the art of conscious creation, teaching them to wield their thoughts and intentions as powerful tools to shape their reality and contribute to the collective evolution.

Harmonia: A gentle soul who carried the frequencies of harmony, peace, and unity. Harmonia guided Liam and Elysia in embracing compassion, empathy, and the interconnectedness of all beings. They discovered that through acts of kindness, love, and service, they could uplift not only their own lives but also the lives of others.

Together, Liam, Elysia, and their fellow spiritual seekers embarked on a transformative journey of self-discovery and expansion of consciousness. They delved into the mysteries of the universe, explored the realms of energy healing and spiritual practices, and deepened their connection to the divine.

In their spiritual odyssey, they witnessed the profound transformations that occurred when beings embraced their spiritual nature. The Astral Sanctuary became a haven of enlightenment, where souls awakened to their true purpose, healed past wounds, and discovered their unique gifts to contribute to the world.

In the climactic moment of their spiritual journey, Liam and Elysia reached the heart of the Astral Sanctuary—an ethereal temple pulsating with divine energy. There, they experienced a profound merging of their individual consciousness with the universal consciousness, transcending the boundaries of time and space.

In this transcendent state, Liam and Elysia became conduits of divine light and love. They radiated their awakened presence, spreading waves of healing, transformation, and spiritual awakening throughout the Astral Sanctuary and beyond. Their very essence became a catalyst for the evolution of consciousness, inspiring others to embrace their own spiritual potential and embark on the path of self-realization.

The novel concludes with Liam and Elysia continuing their spiritual journey within the Astral Sanctuary, forever devoted to the pursuit of higher knowledge and expanded awareness. Their journey becomes a testament to the transformative power of spiritual growth, the eternal nature of the soul, and the infinite possibilities that unfold when beings connect with their divine essence.

THE ASTRAL SANCTUARY: AWAKENING THE SOUL'S DIVINITY

"The Astral Sanctuary: Awakening the Soul's Divinity" is more than a novel—it is an invitation for readers to embark on their own spiritual odyssey, to explore the depths of their inner being, and to embrace the limitless potential of their soul's divinity. Through the extraordinary journey of Liam and Elysia, readers are encouraged to delve into their own spiritual awakening, connect with their inner wisdom, and embrace the boundless love, light, and wisdom that reside within the depths of their being.

As Liam and Elysia delved deeper into the Astral Sanctuary, they discovered a hidden chamber that radiated an otherworldly energy. Curiosity piqued, they cautiously stepped into the chamber, only to find themselves transported to a dimension of pure light and sound.

In this dimension, they encountered celestial beings unlike any they had encountered before. These beings, known as the Luminara, emanated a brilliance that illuminated the vast expanse of the dimension. The Luminara were the guardians of cosmic harmony and the keepers of sacred cosmic frequencies.

Led by the Luminara, Liam and Elysia embarked on a celestial journey through the dimension of light and sound. Each step they took resonated with cosmic vibrations that awakened dormant aspects of their being and expanded their consciousness.

Through their travels, they discovered that this dimension held the key to unlocking the true potential of the human spirit. The Luminara taught Liam and Elysia how to attune themselves to the cosmic frequencies, harmonizing their energy with the divine symphony that permeated all of creation.

Guided by the Luminara, Liam and Elysia encountered celestial instruments and ethereal soundscapes that transported them to realms of heightened awareness and spiritual connection. They learned to use sound as a tool for healing, transformation, and manifestation.

In their celestial odyssey, they discovered the power of sacred chants, mantras, and celestial melodies that resonated deep within their souls. They learned to tap into the vibrational essence of the universe, creating harmonious frequencies that could uplift, heal, and bring about profound shifts in consciousness.

Liam and Elysia also encountered other beings who inhabited the dimension of light and sound:

Melodia: A celestial muse who embodied the power of creativity and artistic expression. Melodia inspired Liam and Elysia to explore their creative potential, using sound, color, and movement as vehicles for self-expression and spiritual growth. They learned that art, in its various forms, had the ability to touch hearts, elevate consciousness, and bridge the realms of the physical and the divine.

Harmonix: A celestial conductor who harmonized the cosmic frequencies and directed the symphony of the universe. Harmonix taught Liam and Elysia the art of divine alignment, helping them attune to the rhythm of the cosmos and find their unique place within the grand orchestration of existence. They learned to embrace the flow of life, trusting in the divine timing and synchronicities that guided their path.

Rhythma: A celestial dancer who embodied the essence of movement and rhythm. Rhythma showed Liam and Elysia the transformative power of dance and physical expression. They discovered that through conscious movement, they could access deep states of presence, connect with their bodies as vessels of divine energy, and cultivate a profound sense of unity with the cosmic dance of life.

Together, Liam, Elysia, and their celestial companions journeyed through the dimension of light and sound, attuning themselves to the cosmic frequencies and exploring the limitless possibilities of divine expression. They immersed themselves in celestial symphonies, danced with the cosmic rhythms, and painted with the colors of the divine palette.

In the climactic moment of their celestial odyssey, Liam and Elysia stood before the Celestial Harmonium—a grand instrument that harnessed the collective frequencies of the cosmos. They united their intentions and created a symphony of love, harmony, and unity that reverberated throughout the dimension of light and sound.

Their celestial composition echoed across the dimensions, touching the hearts of beings in realms beyond their own. It became a clarion call for unity, inviting all beings to embrace their inherent divinity and co-create a world of harmony and love.

The novel concludes with Liam and Elysia continuing their exploration of the dimension of light and sound, forever inspired by the celestial melodies and harmonies they encounter. They become ambassadors of the cosmic symphony, sharing the wisdom and power of sound and vibration with others, and cultivating a world where every being can attune to the frequencies of love and create their own divine melody.

THE CELESTIAL MELODIES: EMBRACING THE HARMONY OF THE UNIVERSE

"The Celestial Melodies: Embracing the Harmony of the Universe" is more than a novel—it is an invitation for readers to embark on their own celestial odyssey, to explore the transformative power of sound, vibration, and creative expression, and to align with the harmonious frequencies that permeate all of creation. Through the extraordinary journey of Liam and Elysia, readers are encouraged to discover their unique place in the cosmic symphony, express their true essence through creativity, and harmonize their lives with the divine rhythm that pulses within their hearts.

As Liam and Elysia delved deeper into the dimension of light and sound, they encountered a portal that shimmered with an ethereal glow. Intrigued, they stepped through the portal and found themselves in a realm where the fabric of reality seemed to ripple with the energy of pure imagination.

In this realm, they discovered a race of celestial beings known as the Illuminari. The Illuminari were radiant beings of light, each carrying a unique essence of creativity and inspiration. They welcomed Liam and Elysia with open arms, inviting them to join in the co-creation of a world where imagination knew no bounds.

Guided by the Illuminari, Liam and Elysia embarked on an extraordinary journey through the realm of boundless imagination. They witnessed breathtaking landscapes that shifted and morphed with the power of their thoughts, where dreams took shape and realities merged. It was a realm where the imagination was the wellspring of creation and every thought held the potential to manifest.

In this wondrous realm, they encountered celestial beings who embodied the essence of imagination:

Lumina: A celestial muse who radiated vibrant colors and inspired the creation of visual art. Lumina guided Liam and Elysia through realms of infinite beauty and encouraged them to unleash their artistic expression. They learned to paint with the hues of their emotions, sculpt with the textures of their dreams, and infuse their creations with the essence of their souls.

Harmonis: A celestial bard who wove melodies with his voice and instrument. Harmonis taught Liam and Elysia the power of music as a language of the soul. They discovered the ability to compose symphonies that resonated with the hearts of all who heard them, evoking emotions, healing wounds, and bridging the gap between realms.

Storya: A celestial storyteller who wove tales with words that transported listeners to realms of wonder and possibility. Storya invited Liam and Elysia to explore the power of storytelling as a means to inspire, educate, and ignite the imagination. They discovered that stories held the potential to shape realities and bridge the realms of the seen and the unseen.

Together, Liam, Elysia, and their celestial companions embarked on a journey of creative exploration and self-discovery. They engaged in the co-creation of magnificent landscapes, invented new languages, and crafted stories that ignited the imagination of all who encountered them.

In their imaginative odyssey, they witnessed the transformative power of their thoughts and intentions. They learned that the boundaries of their world were limited only by their beliefs and that every act of creation had the potential to inspire, uplift, and shape the future.

As they explored the depths of their own imaginations, Liam and Elysia realized that the realm they were traversing was not separate from their physical reality but intricately woven into it. They understood that the power of their imagination extended far beyond the boundaries of their journey, shaping their perception of the world and influencing their experiences.

In the climactic moment of their imaginative odyssey, Liam and Elysia stood at the center of a kaleidoscope of creativity—a place where all forms of artistic expression converged. They joined hands with the Illuminari and created a grand spectacle of music, art, and storytelling that reverberated throughout the realms of existence.

Their co-creation sparked a global awakening of the imagination, inspiring individuals from all walks of life to embrace their creative potential and tap into the limitless power of their own imaginations. The world became a canvas where art flourished, music transcended language, and stories carried the collective wisdom of humanity.

The novel concludes with Liam and Elysia continuing their exploration of the realm of boundless imagination, forever inspired by the beauty and infinite possibilities that it held. They become catalysts for creativity, fostering a world where the arts are celebrated, where imagination is nurtured, and where every individual is encouraged to embrace their unique creative essence.

THE REALM OF INFINITE IMAGINATION: UNLEASHING THE POWER WITHIN

"The Realm of Infinite Imagination: Unleashing the Power Within" is more than a novel—it is an invitation for readers to embark on their own imaginative odyssey, to explore the depths of their creative potential, and to tap into the infinite wellspring of inspiration that resides within them. Through the extraordinary journey of Liam and Elysia, readers are encouraged to unleash their imagination, embrace their unique creative gifts, and co-create a world where the power of the imagination shapes their reality.

As Liam and Elysia continued their exploration of the realm of boundless imagination, they came across a hidden path that led to a mystical garden. The garden overflowed with vibrant flowers, magical creatures, and shimmering streams of pure creative energy. It was a sanctuary where inspiration blossomed and dreams took flight.

In this enchanted garden, they encountered a group of celestial beings known as the Dreamweavers. The Dreamweavers were ethereal beings who harnessed the power of dreams to shape the tapestry of reality. They greeted Liam and Elysia with warmth and wisdom, inviting them to tap into the limitless potential of their dreams.

Guided by the Dreamweavers, Liam and Elysia embarked on a journey through the realm of dreams—a realm where the boundaries of time, space, and possibility were fluid. They witnessed dreams manifesting into tangible realities, explored surreal landscapes, and encountered beings who existed solely within the realm of dreams.

In this fantastical realm, they encountered celestial beings who embodied the essence of dreams:

Celestia: A celestial oracle who had the ability to traverse the realms of dreams and decipher their symbolic messages. Celestia taught Liam and Elysia the language of dreams, helping them uncover hidden meanings, access their subconscious wisdom, and gain clarity and guidance from their dream experiences.

Morpheus: A celestial shapeshifter who could transform into any form within the realm of dreams. Morpheus guided Liam and Elysia through dreamscape adventures, where they discovered the power of lucid dreaming—becoming aware within their dreams and actively shaping the dreamscapes to fulfill their desires and gain deeper insights.

Astralis: A celestial guide who bridged the realms of dreams and waking life, helping Liam and Elysia integrate the wisdom and energy from their dream experiences into their physical reality. Astralis taught them techniques to enhance dream recall, engage in dream journaling, and tap into the creative potential of their dreams.

Together, Liam, Elysia, and their celestial companions ventured deeper into the realm of dreams. They explored dreamscapes of unimaginable beauty, engaged in conversations with dream entities, and unlocked hidden aspects of their own psyche.

In their dream odyssey, they realized that dreams were not merely fleeting illusions but powerful gateways to self-discovery and transformation. They learned to navigate the dream realm with intention, harnessing the energy of their dreams to manifest desired outcomes in their waking lives.

As they delved deeper into their dream experiences, Liam and Elysia discovered a collective dream consciousness—an interconnected web of dreams shared by all beings. They realized that their dreams held the power to influence the collective consciousness and co-create a reality aligned with the highest visions and aspirations of humanity.

In the climactic moment of their dream odyssey, Liam and Elysia found themselves standing at the crossroads of their dreams and waking life. They realized that the two realms were not separate, but intimately connected. They understood that the power of their dreams could inspire and shape their actions in the physical world, creating a ripple effect of positive change.

Their newfound understanding propelled them to become ambassadors of dream consciousness, encouraging others to pay attention to their dreams, explore their inner realms, and harness the transformative power of their dream experiences. They became advocates for dream interpretation, creating workshops and sharing techniques to help individuals unlock the wisdom and healing potential of their dreams.

The novel concludes with Liam and Elysia continuing their exploration of the realm of dreams, forever inspired by the beauty, wisdom, and limitless potential that it holds. They become agents of transformation, guiding others to tap into the profound insights and creative energy available in their dreamscapes, and co-creating a world where dreams are honored as sacred gateways to self-discovery and personal growth.

THE DREAMWEAVERS: AWAKENING THE POWER OF DREAMS

"The Dreamweavers: Awakening the Power of Dreams" is more than a novel—it is an invitation for readers to embark on their own dream odyssey, to embrace the wisdom and healing potential of their dreams, and to co-create a reality that reflects the highest visions of their souls. Through the extraordinary journey of Liam and Elysia, readers are encouraged to explore their dreams, tap into the power of their subconscious mind, and embrace the transformative energy that lies within the realm of dreams.

As Liam and Elysia delved deeper into the realm of dreams, they discovered a hidden portal that shimmered with an iridescent light. Curiosity sparked within them, and they stepped through the portal, finding themselves transported to a dimension where time flowed like a river and the boundaries of past, present, and future dissolved into a timeless tapestry.

In this dimension, they encountered celestial beings known as the Timeweavers. The Timeweavers were beings of infinite wisdom who possessed the ability to navigate the currents of time and guide the unfolding of destiny. They greeted Liam and Elysia with a knowing smile, inviting them to embark on a profound journey through the threads of time.

Guided by the Timeweavers, Liam and Elysia ventured into the realm of temporal exploration. They witnessed pivotal moments in history, experienced glimpses of their own past lives, and observed the probabilities and potentials of the future. They learned that time was not linear but a multidimensional tapestry interwoven with infinite possibilities.

In their temporal odyssey, they encountered celestial beings who embodied the essence of time:

Chronos: A wise and ancient cosmic sage who held the keys to the mysteries of time. Chronos guided Liam and Elysia through the temporal realms, helping them understand the intricate web of cause and effect and the interplay of free will and destiny. They learned to navigate the currents of time, understanding that their choices could shape the trajectory of their own lives and the course of history.

Tempora: A celestial guardian of temporal balance and harmony. Tempora showed Liam and Elysia the delicate dance between past, present, and future, emphasizing the importance of being fully present in the present moment. They learned to embrace the lessons of the past, create consciously in the present, and hold the vision of their desired future.

Kairos: A celestial entity who personified the opportune moment—the "perfect timing" that aligned with the cosmic flow. Kairos guided Liam and Elysia in recognizing and seizing the auspicious moments in their lives. They learned to trust their intuition, follow the signs of synchronicity, and surrender to the divine timing that orchestrated their soul's journey.

Together, Liam, Elysia, and their celestial companions journeyed through the depths of time, witnessing significant historical events, accessing memories from past lives, and glimpsing potential futures. They unraveled the interconnectedness of these temporal threads, realizing that the past, present, and future were intricately interwoven, influencing one another in a dance of cosmic evolution.

As they explored the complexities of time, Liam and Elysia discovered that their journey through time was not merely a passive observation but an active participation in the unfolding of destiny. They understood that their intentions, actions, and choices in the present moment had the power to ripple through time, shaping their own lives and contributing to the collective tapestry of human experience.

In the climactic moment of their temporal odyssey, Liam and Elysia found themselves at a pivotal juncture—a convergence point of multiple timelines. They realized that their journey through time had led them to a crucial moment of choice—one that would have far-reaching consequences not only for themselves but for the entire fabric of existence.

With deep reverence and intention, Liam and Elysia made their choice, guided by the wisdom they had gained from their cosmic journey. They aligned their intentions with the highest good, choosing a path of love, unity, and conscious evolution. Their choice sent ripples through time, shaping a future where humanity awakened to its true potential and lived in harmony with the cosmos.

The novel concludes with Liam and Elysia continuing their journey through time, forever inspired by the profound insights, connections, and revelations that they experienced. They become catalysts for positive change, sharing their wisdom with others, and encouraging individuals to recognize their power to shape their destiny and contribute to the collective evolution of consciousness.

THE THREADS OF TIME: UNRAVELING DESTINY'S TAPESTRY

"The Threads of Time: Unraveling Destiny's Tapestry" is more than a novel—it is an invitation for readers to embark on their own temporal odyssey, to explore the mysteries of time, and to embrace their power to shape their own destiny. Through the extraordinary journey of Liam and Elysia, readers are encouraged to engage with the present moment, honor the lessons of the past, and envision a future that aligns with their deepest aspirations.

As Liam and Elysia continued their journey through the realms of wonder and discovery, they stumbled upon a hidden gateway leading to the realm of the Elemental Essences. Stepping through the gateway, they found themselves immersed in a world pulsating with the raw power of nature and the elemental forces that shaped existence.

In this realm, they encountered celestial beings known as the Elemental Guardians. These ethereal beings embodied the essence of earth, air, fire, and water, each holding a unique aspect of creation and the natural world. The Elemental Guardians welcomed Liam and Elysia with open arms, inviting them to connect with the elemental forces and learn the sacred wisdom they held.

Guided by the Elemental Guardians, Liam and Elysia embarked on an elemental odyssey, venturing into the depths of each elemental realm to understand its essence:

Terra: The guardian of the earth element, Terra revealed the secrets of the land, the vitality of the soil, and the interconnected web of life that thrived upon the earth. Liam and Elysia delved into the rich ecosystems, communing with majestic creatures, and learning to cultivate harmony with nature.

Zephyr: The guardian of the air element, Zephyr taught Liam and Elysia the power of breath, wind, and the unseen currents of energy. They soared through the skies, connecting with the wisdom of the avian beings, and honed their intuition, harnessing the gentle force of the wind to navigate life's challenges.

Pyrra: The guardian of the fire element, Pyrra ignited the flames of passion, transformation, and illumination within Liam and Elysia. They delved into the forge of inner alchemy, learning to transmute challenges into opportunities, ignite their creative spark, and embody the radiant warmth of the divine fire within.

Aqua: The guardian of the water element, Aqua immersed Liam and Elysia in the fluid realm of emotions, intuition, and the ever-flowing cycles of life. They dived into the depths of ancient seas, connecting with the wisdom of aquatic creatures, and learned to navigate the currents of their own emotions with grace and understanding.

Together, Liam, Elysia, and their celestial companions ventured deeper into the elemental realms. They witnessed the harmonious interplay of the elemental forces, observed the cycles of creation and transformation, and gained profound insights into the balance and interconnectedness of all life.

In their elemental odyssey, they discovered that the wisdom of the elements extended beyond the physical realm. They realized that the elements resided within them, reflecting the qualities of earth, air, fire, and water in their own beings. They learned to cultivate a harmonious relationship with the elemental essences, honoring and embodying their unique qualities.

As they deepened their connection with the elemental forces, Liam and Elysia discovered their capacity to co-create with nature and become stewards of the Earth. They understood the importance of living in harmony with the natural world, preserving its beauty, and nurturing its delicate ecosystems.

In the climactic moment of their elemental odyssey, Liam and Elysia found themselves at the convergence of all four elemental realms. They realized that the key to true harmony lay in embracing the interplay of the elements within themselves and in their external environment.

With a profound sense of reverence, Liam and Elysia invoked the elemental essences, calling upon the power of earth, air, fire, and water to merge within them. They became vessels of the divine alchemy, embodying the harmonious dance of the elements and radiating their balanced energy throughout the realms.

Their embodiment of the elemental essences ignited a collective awakening, inspiring individuals to reconnect with the natural world, honor the elements, and forge a symbiotic relationship with the Earth. The world became a sanctuary of harmony, where humanity and nature coexisted in balance and reverence.

The novel concludes with Liam and Elysia continuing their exploration of the elemental realms, forever inspired by the wisdom and beauty that nature held. They become guardians of the Earth, spreading awareness and nurturing the collective consciousness towards ecological sustainability and the preservation of the natural world.

THE ELEMENTAL HARMONIES: EMBRACING THE SACRED DANCE OF CREATION

"The Elemental Harmonies: Embracing the Sacred Dance of Creation" is more than a novel—it is an invitation for readers to embark on their own elemental odyssey, to reconnect with the forces of nature, and to embrace their role as stewards of the Earth. Through the extraordinary journey of Liam and Elysia, readers are encouraged to honor the elemental essences within and around them, and to live in harmony with the natural world, fostering a future where humanity and nature thrive as interconnected partners in creation.

As Liam and Elysia continued their journey through the realms of wonder and discovery, they came across a mystical portal pulsating with a vibrant energy. Intrigued, they stepped through the portal, finding themselves in a realm where the boundaries of the physical and the spiritual intertwined—an ethereal realm known as the Celestial Nexus.

In the Celestial Nexus, they encountered celestial beings of pure light and wisdom, known as the Luminara. The Luminara radiated a luminous glow and emanated a profound sense of peace and harmony. They welcomed Liam and Elysia with open hearts, inviting them to explore the mysteries of the celestial realms and delve into the depths of cosmic consciousness.

Guided by the Luminara, Liam and Elysia embarked on a celestial odyssey, venturing into the realms of cosmic knowledge and spiritual awakening. They witnessed the birth of stars, traversed celestial pathways, and communed with celestial entities who held the wisdom of the ages.

In their celestial odyssey, they encountered celestial beings who embodied the essence of cosmic consciousness:

Solara: A radiant being who personified the energy of the sun and the cosmic life force. Solara guided Liam and Elysia in harnessing the power of solar energy, allowing them to tap into their inner vitality and ignite their spiritual awakening. They learned to bask in the light of their own divine essence and radiate love and compassion to all beings.

Luna: A gentle being who personified the energy of the moon and the intuitive realms. Luna helped Liam and Elysia attune to the cycles of nature, guiding them to listen to their inner wisdom and connect with the subtle energies of the universe. They learned to trust their intuition, navigate the ebb and flow of life, and uncover the hidden truths that resided in the depths of their souls.

Aetherius: A wise entity who embodied the energy of the cosmos and the interconnectedness of all things. Aetherius guided Liam and Elysia in expanding their consciousness beyond the confines of their individual selves, allowing them to embrace the unity and oneness of all existence. They learned to perceive the divine interplay of light and darkness, joy and sorrow, and to embrace the inherent divinity in every being they encountered.

Together, Liam, Elysia, and their celestial companions delved deeper into the celestial realms. They traversed celestial pathways, witnessed cosmic events of awe-inspiring magnitude, and unraveled the intricate tapestry of the universe.

In their celestial odyssey, they discovered that the celestial realms were not separate from their own being but intricately connected to their essence. They realized that the wisdom of the cosmos resided within them, waiting to be awakened and integrated into their everyday lives.

As they deepened their connection with cosmic consciousness, Liam and Elysia experienced profound spiritual transformation. They shed limiting beliefs, expanded their perception of reality, and embraced their true nature as divine beings of light.

In the climactic moment of their celestial odyssey, Liam and Elysia found themselves in the heart of the Celestial Nexus—a place where the energy of love and wisdom pulsed with unmatched intensity. They merged with the cosmic essence, experiencing a profound union with the infinite intelligence of the universe.

Their merging with cosmic consciousness awakened a deep sense of purpose within Liam and Elysia. They became conduits of divine light, sharing their newfound wisdom and love with others, and inspiring a collective awakening to the infinite possibilities of cosmic consciousness.

The novel concludes with Liam and Elysia continuing their exploration of the celestial realms, forever inspired by the boundless wisdom and love that they have discovered. They become beacons of light, guiding others on their spiritual journeys, and co-creating a world where humanity embraces its inherent divinity and lives in harmony with the cosmic rhythms of existence.

THE CELESTIAL NEXUS: EMBRACING THE COSMIC TAPESTRY

"The Celestial Nexus: Embracing the Cosmic Tapestry" is more than a novel—it is an invitation for readers to embark on their own celestial odyssey, to awaken to the wisdom of the cosmos, and to embrace their divine essence. Through the extraordinary journey of Liam and Elysia, readers are encouraged to connect with the infinite intelligence of the universe, expand their consciousness, and radiate love and light to all beings.

As Liam and Elysia delved deeper into the celestial realms, they encountered a hidden chamber pulsating with an ethereal light. Curiosity tingled within them, and they cautiously stepped into the chamber, feeling a surge of energy envelop them. The chamber was a gateway to a realm beyond their wildest imagination—a realm known as the Luminous Void.

In the Luminous Void, they found themselves surrounded by an expanse of pure light, devoid of form and boundaries. It was a realm where all possibilities converged and the essence of creation itself resided. In this mystical realm, they encountered celestial beings known as the Luminalis, beings of pure consciousness and unlimited potential.

Guided by the Luminalis, Liam and Elysia embarked on an extraordinary journey through the Luminous Void. They traversed realms of pure thought and expanded their consciousness to embrace the boundless nature of existence. They witnessed the birth of galaxies, explored cosmic mysteries, and connected with the infinite intelligence that wove through the fabric of the universe.

In their odyssey through the Luminous Void, they encountered celestial beings who embodied the essence of cosmic consciousness:

Zenith: A being of serene wisdom who emanated tranquility and clarity. Zenith guided Liam and Elysia in mastering the art of stillness, helping them quiet their minds and access deeper states of awareness. They learned to transcend the limitations of thought and experience a profound sense of oneness with all that is.

Aurora: A luminescent entity who radiated joy and creativity. Aurora inspired Liam and Elysia to embrace the power of imagination and the creative potential within them. They learned to manifest their desires by aligning their thoughts and intentions with the limitless possibilities of the universe.

Eon: A timeless being who embodied the eternal nature of existence. Eon guided Liam and Elysia in understanding the cycles of creation and dissolution that shaped the cosmos. They learned to flow with the rhythms of change and embrace the impermanence of all things, finding solace in the eternal essence that transcended the temporal.

Together, Liam, Elysia, and their celestial companions ventured deeper into the Luminous Void. They merged with the cosmic consciousness, experienced profound states of unity and bliss, and unraveled the deepest mysteries of existence.

In their odyssey through the Luminous Void, they discovered that they were not separate from the universe but an integral part of it. They realized that their thoughts, intentions, and consciousness had the power to shape their reality and co-create with the cosmic intelligence that permeated all of existence.

As they embraced their connection with cosmic consciousness, Liam and Elysia experienced a profound shift in their perception of self and the world around them. They transcended the limitations of their individual identities and recognized their oneness with all beings. They became instruments of divine expression, channels for the cosmic energy to flow through and create positive transformation.

In the climactic moment of their journey through the Luminous Void, Liam and Elysia found themselves in the heart of the cosmic expanse—a place where the energy of love, wisdom, and pure potentiality pulsed with unmatched intensity. They merged with the essence of the Luminous Void, experiencing a profound union with the infinite intelligence of the cosmos.

Their merging with cosmic consciousness ignited a profound awakening within Liam and Elysia. They became ambassadors of divine light, sharing their expanded wisdom and love with others, and inspiring a collective shift in consciousness. They realized that they were the authors of their own reality and that by aligning their thoughts and intentions with the highest good, they could create a world filled with love, harmony, and infinite possibilities.

The novel concludes with Liam and Elysia continuing their exploration of the Luminous Void, forever inspired by the boundless wisdom and love they have discovered. They become catalysts for spiritual growth and transformation, guiding others to awaken to their true nature as divine beings of light and to co-create a reality aligned with the highest vision of humanity.

THE LUMINOUS VOID: AWAKENING THE INFINITE WITHIN

"The Luminous Void: Awakening the Infinite Within" is more than a novel—it is an invitation for readers to embark on their own cosmic odyssey, to explore the depths of their consciousness, and to embrace their infinite potential. Through the extraordinary journey of Liam and Elysia, readers are encouraged to connect with the cosmic intelligence, expand their awareness, and radiate love and light to all beings.

As Liam and Elysia continued their exploration of the Luminous Void, they encountered a radiant celestial gateway that beckoned them further into the mysteries of the cosmos. With a sense of awe and anticipation, they stepped through the gateway and found themselves in a realm beyond comprehension—a realm known as the Celestial Harmony.

In the Celestial Harmony, they were enveloped by a symphony of divine energies, resonating in perfect harmony. The realm pulsed with celestial melodies and ethereal colors, creating a tapestry of beauty that transcended the boundaries of imagination. It was a realm where the vibrations of love, compassion, and unity reverberated throughout every particle of existence.

In this transcendent realm, they encountered celestial beings known as the Harmonia. The Harmonia were embodiments of divine harmony and grace, radiating an aura of unconditional love and understanding. They welcomed

Liam and Elysia with open arms, inviting them to immerse themselves in the sacred dance of celestial harmony.

Guided by the Harmonia, Liam and Elysia embarked on a celestial odyssey through the realms of harmonious existence. They witnessed the interplay of energies, the convergence of light and sound, and the profound interconnectedness of all things. They learned that true harmony was not the absence of conflict but the understanding and integration of polarities.

In their celestial odyssey, they encountered celestial beings who embodied the essence of celestial harmony:

Melodia: A celestial muse who emanated melodies of divine harmony. Melodia guided Liam and Elysia to attune their hearts to the celestial symphony, teaching them to listen deeply to the inner rhythms and harmonies of their own souls. They learned to express their authentic voices, using music as a medium to heal, inspire, and uplift.

Seraphine: A celestial healer who channeled the energies of harmony and balance. Seraphine introduced Liam and Elysia to the art of energetic healing, teaching them to align their energies with the celestial harmonies and restore balance within themselves and the world around them. They learned to heal through the power of love and became vessels of divine harmony.

Equinox: A celestial guide who personified the balance between light and dark, day and night. Equinox guided Liam and Elysia to embrace the interplay of polarities, helping them recognize the beauty and wisdom that resided within contrasting forces. They learned to find equilibrium within themselves and honor the inherent balance that existed in the universe.

Together, Liam, Elysia, and their celestial companions ventured deeper into the realms of celestial harmony. They immersed themselves in the cosmic dance of light and sound, experiencing moments of transcendence where time and space dissolved, and the essence of divine harmony permeated their being.

In their celestial odyssey, they discovered that harmony was not something to be achieved solely on an individual level but was a collective endeavor. They realized that by radiating their own harmonious energies, they could inspire others to find their own unique harmony and create a harmonious tapestry of interconnected souls.

As they deepened their connection with celestial harmony, Liam and Elysia experienced a profound shift in their perception of self and others. They embraced the inherent unity that underlies all of existence and recognized that every being held a unique part in the symphony of life. They became conduits of divine harmony, extending love, compassion, and understanding to all beings they encountered.

In the climactic moment of their celestial odyssey, Liam and Elysia found themselves in the heart of the Celestial Harmony—a place where the energies of love, compassion, and unity merged into an exquisite symphony. They merged with the essence of celestial harmony, experiencing a profound union with the divine vibrations of the universe.

Their merging with celestial harmony awakened a deep sense of purpose within Liam and Elysia. They became ambassadors of divine love and harmony, sharing their expanded wisdom and radiating their harmonious energies to others. They realized that their actions, thoughts, and intentions had the power to ripple through the collective consciousness, creating a harmonious and compassionate world.

The novel concludes with Liam and Elysia continuing their exploration of the Celestial Harmony, forever inspired by the profound beauty and wisdom they have discovered. They become catalysts for unity, guiding others on their journey towards inner harmony and co-creating a reality where love, compassion, and understanding are the guiding principles.

THE CELESTIAL HARMONY: EMBRACING THE SYMPHONY OF LIFE

"The Celestial Harmony: Embracing the Symphony of Life" is more than a novel—it is an invitation for readers to embark on their own celestial odyssey, to attune their hearts to the divine harmonies, and to radiate love and compassion to all beings. Through the extraordinary journey of Liam and Elysia, readers are encouraged to recognize the inherent unity in all of existence, harmonize their inner energies, and co-create a world where harmony and compassion prevail.

As Liam and Elysia continued their exploration of the Celestial Harmony, they felt a gentle pull toward a radiant archway adorned with symbols of interconnectedness and unity. Curiosity ignited within them, and they stepped through the archway, finding themselves in a realm that shimmered with pure love—a realm known as the Divine Heart.

In the Divine Heart, they were embraced by an all-encompassing love that transcended comprehension. The realm emanated an energy of pure compassion, acceptance, and interconnectedness. It was a realm where the divine essence of every being was recognized and honored, and the unity of all creation was celebrated.

In this sacred realm, they encountered celestial beings known as the Amara. The Amara were beings of pure love and compassion, radiating a divine presence that enveloped Liam and Elysia with an overwhelming sense of peace and acceptance. They welcomed them with open hearts, inviting them to delve into the depths of the Divine Heart and discover the transformative power of love.

Guided by the Amara, Liam and Elysia embarked on a transcendent odyssey through the realms of divine love. They witnessed the unending compassion that flowed from the Divine Heart, experienced the interconnectedness of all souls, and delved into the transformative power of forgiveness and acceptance.

In their celestial odyssey, they encountered celestial beings who embodied the essence of divine love:

Amara: The celestial guardians of the Divine Heart. The Amara taught Liam and Elysia the art of unconditional love and acceptance. They learned to embrace the divine essence within themselves and all beings, transcending judgment and embracing the interconnectedness of all souls.

Seraphiel: A radiant being who embodied the transformative power of forgiveness. Seraphiel guided Liam and Elysia in releasing past hurts, embracing forgiveness, and nurturing compassion toward themselves and others. They learned to heal emotional wounds through the power of forgiveness and discovered that forgiveness was an act of liberation and an expression of divine love.

Anahita: A celestial guide who personified the divine feminine energy of nurturing and compassion. Anahita helped Liam and Elysia tap into their own nurturing qualities, encouraging them to cultivate self-love and extend compassion to themselves and others. They learned that true strength and empowerment came from embracing the nurturing qualities within their hearts.

Together, Liam, Elysia, and their celestial companions journeyed deeper into the realms of divine love. They bathed in the radiant energy of the Divine Heart, embraced the interconnectedness of all souls, and discovered the transformative power of love and compassion.

In their celestial odyssey, they discovered that divine love was not an abstract concept but a tangible force that had the power to heal, transform, and elevate consciousness. They realized that love was the very essence of their being and the source from which all creation emerged.

As they deepened their connection with divine love, Liam and Elysia experienced a profound shift in their perception of themselves and the world. They recognized that love was not limited to romantic or familial relationships but extended to all beings and the entire universe. They became beacons of divine love, radiating compassion, acceptance, and kindness wherever they went.

In the climactic moment of their celestial odyssey, Liam and Elysia found themselves at the center of the Divine Heart—a place where the energies of love and unity merged into a sublime symphony. They merged with the essence of divine love, experiencing a profound union with the infinite wellspring of love that flowed through all existence.

Their merging with divine love awakened a deep sense of purpose within Liam and Elysia. They became emissaries of divine love, sharing their expanded wisdom and radiating love and compassion to all beings. They realized that every thought, word, and action infused with love had the power to create a ripple effect of healing and transformation in the world.

The novel concludes with Liam and Elysia continuing their exploration of the Divine Heart, forever inspired by the boundless love and compassion they have discovered. They become catalysts for unity and healing, guiding others on their journey to rediscover their own divine essence and co-create a reality where love is the guiding force.

THE DIVINE HEART: EMBRACING THE POWER OF LOVE

"The Divine Heart: Embracing the Power of Love" is more than a novel—it is an invitation for readers to embark on their own transformative odyssey, to open their hearts to the infinite wellspring of love within and around them, and to radiate compassion, acceptance, and kindness to all beings. Through the extraordinary journey of Liam and Elysia, readers are encouraged to recognize their own divine essence, nurture their capacity for love and forgiveness, and co-create a world where love is the foundation for all interactions and relationships.

As Liam and Elysia continued their exploration of the Divine Heart, they felt a gentle pull toward a serene garden bathed in a soft, golden light. Intrigued, they followed the calling and entered the garden, discovering a realm of profound peace and tranquility—a realm known as the Serenity Garden.

In the Serenity Garden, they were surrounded by lush foliage, vibrant flowers, and the gentle sound of flowing water. The air was filled with a sense of calm and serenity that enveloped their souls. It was a realm where the harmony of nature and the inner peace of the heart merged into a tranquil oasis.

In this sacred realm, they encountered celestial beings known as the Seraphim. The Seraphim emanated an ethereal presence, embodying the essence of serenity and inner stillness. They welcomed Liam and Elysia with open arms, inviting them to immerse themselves in the serenity of the garden and discover the transformative power of inner peace.

Guided by the Seraphim, Liam and Elysia embarked on a contemplative odyssey through the realms of serenity and inner stillness. They learned the art of mindful presence, delved into the depths of meditation, and connected with the profound peace that resided within their own beings.

In their celestial odyssey, they encountered celestial beings who embodied the essence of serenity:

Seraphina: A serene being who emanated a tranquil presence. Seraphina guided Liam and Elysia in the practice of mindfulness and the art of being fully present in the here and now. They learned to quiet their minds, embrace the beauty of the present moment, and cultivate inner stillness amidst the busyness of life.

Solace: A gentle entity who personified solace and comfort. Solace provided Liam and Elysia with a safe space to retreat and find solace in times of challenge or emotional turmoil. They learned to embrace the healing power of solitude, reconnect with their inner selves, and find strength in the serenity that resided within.

Tranquilis: A serene guide who embodied the power of harmonizing emotions. Tranquilis taught Liam and Elysia the art of emotional balance and the importance of cultivating inner peace amidst the turbulence of emotions. They learned to navigate the waves of their feelings with grace and find equilibrium in the depths of their hearts.

Together, Liam, Elysia, and their celestial companions ventured deeper into the realms of serenity. They wandered through the gardens, meditated in serene alcoves, and discovered the transformative power of inner peace.

In their celestial odyssey, they discovered that serenity was not the absence of external disturbances but a state of being that could be cultivated within. They realized that true peace resided in the depths of their own hearts, and they carried that peace with them wherever they went.

As they deepened their connection with serenity, Liam and Elysia experienced a profound shift in their perception of themselves and the world. They recognized that true peace came from within, and they became the calm amidst the storm. They radiated serenity and tranquility, offering solace and inspiration to those around them.

In the climactic moment of their celestial odyssey, Liam and Elysia found themselves at the heart of the Serenity Garden—a place where the energies of peace, tranquility, and stillness merged into a serene symphony. They merged with the essence of serenity, experiencing a profound union with the inner peace that permeated all of existence.

Their merging with serenity awakened a deep sense of purpose within Liam and Elysia. They became ambassadors of inner peace, sharing their expanded wisdom and radiating serenity to all beings. They realized that the cultivation of inner peace had the power to create ripples of harmony and compassion in the world.

The novel concludes with Liam and Elysia continuing their exploration of the Serenity Garden, forever inspired by the profound peace and tranquility they have discovered. They become catalysts for inner harmony and stillness, guiding others on their journey toward inner peace and co-creating a reality where serenity is embraced.

THE SERENITY GARDEN: CULTIVATING INNER PEACE

"The Serenity Garden: Cultivating Inner Peace" is more than a novel—it is an invitation for readers to embark on their own transformative odyssey, to discover the profound peace that resides within, and to radiate serenity and tranquility to all beings. Through the extraordinary journey of Liam and Elysia, readers are encouraged to cultivate inner stillness, find solace amidst the chaos of life, and co-create a world where peace and serenity prevail.

As Liam and Elysia continued their exploration of the Serenity Garden, they were drawn towards a shimmering waterfall that cascaded with pure light. Intrigued by its radiant beauty, they approached the waterfall and discovered a hidden passage behind the curtain of water—a passage that led to a realm of profound wisdom and enlightenment—a realm known as the Illuminated Path.

In the Illuminated Path, they found themselves in a realm of infinite knowledge and heightened consciousness. The air crackled with the energy of wisdom, and the surroundings glowed with the light of profound understanding. It was a realm where ancient teachings and celestial wisdom converged, offering guidance and illumination to those who sought truth.

In this sacred realm, they encountered celestial beings known as the Luminary Sages. The Luminary Sages emanated an aura of wisdom and enlightenment, embodying the essence of cosmic knowledge and divine insight. They welcomed Liam and Elysia with open hearts, inviting them to embark on a journey of inner illumination and discover the depths of their own wisdom.

Guided by the Luminary Sages, Liam and Elysia embarked on a transformative odyssey along the Illuminated Path. They traversed realms of ancient wisdom, delved into the mysteries of existence, and awakened to the profound truths that lay within their own beings.

In their celestial odyssey, they encountered celestial beings who embodied the essence of wisdom and enlightenment:

Orion: A celestial sage who radiated profound insight and cosmic understanding. Orion guided Liam and Elysia in unraveling the mysteries of the universe, expanding their awareness, and deepening their understanding of the interconnectedness of all things. They learned to perceive reality from a higher perspective and embrace the wisdom that resided within.

Sophia: A luminous entity who personified divine wisdom and the awakening of consciousness. Sophia nurtured Liam and Elysia's intellectual and spiritual growth, illuminating the path of self-discovery and guiding them to access their innate wisdom. They learned to integrate the knowledge they acquired with the wisdom of their hearts, becoming vessels of enlightened understanding.

Metatron: An ancient sage who embodied the harmonization of knowledge and spiritual experience. Metatron taught Liam and Elysia to bridge the gap between theory and practice, helping them integrate wisdom into their daily lives. They learned to embody the teachings they encountered, nurturing a deep sense of authenticity and integrity on their spiritual journey.

Together, Liam, Elysia, and their celestial companions journeyed deeper into the realms of wisdom and enlightenment. They immersed themselves in sacred texts, engaged in profound dialogues, and uncovered the profound truths that resonated within their own souls.

In their celestial odyssey, they discovered that wisdom was not confined to external sources but a profound knowing that resided within. They realized that true enlightenment came from the integration of knowledge and personal experience, and the alignment of the mind, heart, and spirit.

As they deepened their connection with wisdom and enlightenment, Liam and Elysia experienced a profound shift in their perception of themselves and the world. They recognized that they were vessels of cosmic wisdom, carrying within them the keys to unlock profound understanding and guide others on their own paths of illumination.

In the climactic moment of their celestial odyssey, Liam and Elysia found themselves at the heart of the Illuminated Path—a place where the energies of wisdom and enlightenment merged into a celestial symphony. They merged with the essence of cosmic knowledge, experiencing a profound union with the infinite wisdom that permeated all of existence.

Their merging with wisdom and enlightenment awakened a deep sense of purpose within Liam and Elysia. They became luminaries of knowledge, sharing their expanded wisdom and guiding others on their journey toward self-discovery and illumination. They realized that the quest for wisdom was never-ending and that true enlightenment was found in the continual exploration and growth of the soul.

The novel concludes with Liam and Elysia continuing their exploration of the Illuminated Path, forever inspired by the profound wisdom and enlightenment they have discovered. They become beacons of cosmic knowledge, sharing their insights and illuminating the paths of others, co-creating a reality where wisdom and enlightenment are cherished.

THE ILLUMINATED PATH: JOURNEY TO COSMIC WISDOM

"The Illuminated Path: Journey to Cosmic Wisdom" is more than a novel—it is an invitation for readers to embark on their own transformative odyssey, to embrace the depths of their inner wisdom, and to radiate enlightenment to all beings. Through the extraordinary journey of Liam and Elysia, readers are encouraged to explore the realms of knowledge and illumination, integrate wisdom into their lives, and co-create a world where wisdom and enlightenment guide the evolution of consciousness.

As Liam and Elysia continued their exploration of the Illuminated Path, they came upon a sacred library that stretched as far as the eye could see. The shelves were filled with ancient tomes, scrolls, and sacred texts—a treasure trove of knowledge waiting to be discovered. Intrigued by the wealth of wisdom contained within, they entered the library and felt a surge of reverence wash over them.

In the library, they encountered celestial beings known as the Librarians of Eternity. The Librarians were guardians of knowledge, with ethereal forms that glowed with a radiant light. They welcomed Liam and Elysia with warm smiles, inviting them to delve into the vast archives of the library and uncover the secrets that lay hidden within the ancient texts.

Guided by the Librarians of Eternity, Liam and Elysia embarked on a profound journey of exploration and discovery. They immersed themselves in the wisdom of the ages, studying the teachings of sages, mystics, and visionaries who had walked the path before them. They delved into the realms of philosophy, spirituality, science, and art, expanding their minds and nurturing their souls with the profound knowledge contained within the sacred texts.

In their celestial odyssey, they encountered celestial beings who embodied the essence of knowledge and wisdom:

Aurelia: A celestial sage who possessed an encyclopedic knowledge of history, philosophy, and culture. Aurelia guided Liam and Elysia through the vast library, sharing insights and stories that illuminated the interconnectedness of human experience across time and space. They learned to embrace the wisdom held within the tapestry of human history and recognize the universal truths that transcended individual perspectives.

Prometheus: A wise being who possessed a deep understanding of science, technology, and the mysteries of the universe. Prometheus ignited Liam and Elysia's curiosity about the cosmos, revealing the wonders of the natural world and the intricate mechanisms that governed its workings. They learned to appreciate the harmony between scientific inquiry and spiritual exploration, recognizing that both paths led to a deeper understanding of the mysteries of existence.

Calliope: A celestial muse who embodied the essence of art, literature, and creativity. Calliope inspired Liam and Elysia to explore the realms of imagination and express their insights through various forms of artistic expression. They learned that art had the power to transcend words and touch the deepest recesses of the human soul, allowing for a profound connection to the realms of wisdom and inspiration.

Together, Liam, Elysia, and their celestial companions delved deeper into the realms of knowledge and understanding. They uncovered hidden truths, connected with the wisdom of the ages, and synthesized their newfound knowledge with their own experiences and insights.

In their celestial odyssey, they discovered that knowledge was not simply a collection of facts, but a transformative force that expanded their perception of reality. They realized that true wisdom came from integrating knowledge with their own lived experiences, allowing for a deeper understanding of themselves, others, and the universe at large.

As they deepened their connection with knowledge and wisdom, Liam and Elysia experienced a profound shift in their perception of themselves and the world. They recognized that they were custodians of knowledge and wisdom, responsible for sharing their insights and inspiring others to embark on their own journeys of discovery. They became vessels of wisdom, guiding others to explore the vast library of existence and find the answers that resonated within their own hearts.

In the climactic moment of their celestial odyssey, Liam and Elysia found themselves at the heart of the library—a place where the energies of knowledge and wisdom merged into a symphony of illumination. They merged with the essence of profound understanding, experiencing a profound union with the infinite wellspring of knowledge that flowed through all of existence.

Their merging with knowledge and wisdom awakened a deep sense of purpose within Liam and Elysia. They became ambassadors of wisdom, sharing their expanded knowledge and guiding others on their own paths of discovery and enlightenment. They recognized that knowledge was a gift meant to be shared and used for the betterment of all beings.

The novel concludes with Liam and Elysia continuing their exploration of the library, forever inspired by the vast knowledge and wisdom they have discovered. They become stewards of wisdom, guiding others on their quests for knowledge and co-creating a reality where wisdom and understanding are cherished.

THE LIBRARY OF ETERNITY: UNVEILING THE SECRETS OF THE AGES

"The Library of Eternity: Unveiling the Secrets of the Ages" is more than a novel—it is an invitation for readers to embark on their own transformative odyssey, to explore the realms of knowledge and understanding, and to share their wisdom with the world. Through the extraordinary journey of Liam and Elysia, readers are encouraged to embrace the power of knowledge, nurture their curiosity, and co-create a world where wisdom and understanding guide the path to a brighter future.

As Liam and Elysia continued their exploration of the Library of Eternity, they discovered a hidden chamber tucked away in a secluded corner. Intrigued by its mysterious aura, they entered the chamber and found themselves in a realm that resonated with pure inspiration—a realm known as the Realm of Imagination.

In the Realm of Imagination, the air was charged with creative energy, and vibrant colors danced before their eyes. It was a realm where possibilities were endless, where dreams took shape, and where the boundaries of reality blurred. Here, the power of imagination held sway, inviting Liam and Elysia to unleash their creative potential and co-create a world beyond their wildest dreams.

In this sacred realm, they encountered celestial beings known as the Muse Guardians. The Muse Guardians were embodiments of inspiration and creativity, radiating an otherworldly glow that sparked the imagination. They welcomed Liam and Elysia with open arms, inviting them to tap into the wellspring of their creative essence and embrace the boundless realms of artistic expression.

Guided by the Muse Guardians, Liam and Elysia embarked on a wondrous odyssey through the realms of imagination and creativity. They engaged in artistic endeavors, explored various forms of expression, and allowed their imaginations to soar to new heights. They discovered that within the depths of their own being lay the power to shape and manifest their most cherished visions.

In their celestial odyssey, they encountered celestial beings who embodied the essence of imagination and creativity:

Lyra: A celestial poet who wove words into enchanting tapestries of emotion and meaning. Lyra encouraged Liam and Elysia to express their innermost thoughts and feelings through the power of language and verse. They learned to harness the magic of words, painting vivid landscapes of the heart and soul.

Apollo: A celestial musician who emanated melodies that touched the deepest realms of the soul. Apollo inspired Liam and Elysia to channel their emotions and thoughts into musical compositions that resonated with the universe. They learned to create symphonies that stirred hearts and awakened dormant emotions.

Chroma: A celestial artist who splashed colors upon the canvas of existence. Chroma encouraged Liam and Elysia to embrace the world of visual arts, unlocking their hidden talents and allowing their imaginations to breathe life into vivid masterpieces. They learned to manifest their inner visions in tangible form, creating art that evoked awe and stirred the soul.

Together, Liam, Elysia, and their celestial companions ventured deeper into the realms of imagination and creativity. They explored the landscapes of dreams, painted with the hues of inspiration, and breathed life into their wildest fantasies.

In their celestial odyssey, they discovered that the power of imagination was not confined to the realm of dreams but held the potential to shape their reality. They realized that creativity was an inherent aspect of their being, a divine spark that allowed them to co-create with the universe and bring forth beauty and innovation.

As they deepened their connection with imagination and creativity, Liam and Elysia experienced a profound shift in their perception of themselves and the world. They recognized that they were co-creators of their reality, and their thoughts and actions held the power to shape the world around them. They became channels for divine inspiration, allowing the Muse Guardians to guide their creative expressions and bring forth their unique gifts to the world.

In the climactic moment of their celestial odyssey, Liam and Elysia found themselves at the heart of the Realm of Imagination—a place where the energies of inspiration and creativity merged into a symphony of boundless possibilities. They merged with the essence of pure imagination, experiencing a profound union with the infinite wellspring of creativity that flowed through all of existence.

Their merging with imagination and creativity awakened a deep sense of purpose within Liam and Elysia. They became custodians of inspiration, sharing their expanded creativity and guiding others on their own journeys of artistic exploration and self-expression. They realized that art and imagination had the power to bridge gaps, transcend boundaries, and unite humanity in a tapestry of diverse and harmonious expressions.

The novel concludes with Liam and Elysia continuing their exploration of the Realm of Imagination, forever inspired by the limitless potential and beauty they have discovered. They become catalysts for creative transformation, nurturing the creative spark in others and co-creating a reality where imagination flourishes.

THE REALM OF IMAGINATION: EMBRACING THE POWER OF CREATIVITY

"The Realm of Imagination: Embracing the Power of Creativity" is more than a novel—it is an invitation for readers to embark on their own transformative odyssey, to tap into the wellspring of their imagination, and to embrace their creative potential. Through the extraordinary journey of Liam and Elysia, readers are encouraged to unlock their unique gifts, express their inner visions, and co-create a world where art, innovation, and imagination thrive.

As Liam and Elysia continued their exploration of the Realm of Imagination, they were drawn to a mysterious portal that shimmered with an ethereal light. Entranced by its allure, they approached the portal and felt a surge of anticipation. With a shared glance, they stepped through the portal, embarking on a journey that would take them beyond the boundaries of their known reality.

They found themselves in a realm where the fabric of time and space seemed to bend and weave in a mesmerizing dance. It was a realm known as the Infinite Tapestry—a place where past, present, and future converged, and the threads of existence intertwined to form a grand tapestry of cosmic interconnectedness.

In the Infinite Tapestry, they encountered celestial beings known as the Weavers of Destiny. The Weavers were masters of cosmic design, able to perceive the intricate patterns of existence and guide the threads of destiny. They welcomed Liam and Elysia with knowing smiles, inviting them to explore the limitless possibilities woven into the fabric of the universe.

Guided by the Weavers of Destiny, Liam and Elysia embarked on an extraordinary odyssey through the realms of time, fate, and purpose. They witnessed the interplay of cause and effect, glimpsed alternate timelines, and discovered the profound influence they held in shaping their own destinies.

In their celestial odyssey, they encountered celestial beings who embodied the essence of destiny and purpose:

Celestia: A celestial oracle who possessed the ability to glimpse the tapestry of fate. Celestia guided Liam and Elysia through the complexities of their personal destinies, illuminating the choices and possibilities that lay before them. They learned to listen to the whispers of their souls and embrace their unique paths with courage and clarity.

Astraeus: A wise being who personified the connection between cosmic cycles and individual growth. Astraeus taught Liam and Elysia to attune to the rhythms of the universe, recognizing the ebb and flow of their own lives within the greater cosmic dance. They learned to navigate the cycles of change with grace and resilience, trusting in the inherent wisdom of the unfolding journey.

Nexus: A celestial guide who embodied the convergence of multiple timelines and parallel realities. Nexus opened Liam and Elysia's awareness to the infinite possibilities that existed beyond their immediate perception. They learned to embrace the power of choice, realizing that every decision had the potential to shape their reality and influence the tapestry of existence.

Together, Liam, Elysia, and their celestial companions delved deeper into the realms of destiny and purpose. They unraveled the threads of their own stories, explored the intricate connections that bound them to others, and discovered the profound impact their actions had on the larger tapestry of life.

In their celestial odyssey, they discovered that destiny was not a fixed path carved in stone, but a fluid interplay between personal choice and cosmic design. They realized that purpose was not something to be discovered, but something to be actively co-created with the universe through conscious intention and aligned action.

As they deepened their connection with destiny and purpose, Liam and Elysia experienced a profound shift in their perception of themselves and the world. They recognized that they were the weavers of their own stories, the architects of their own destinies. They became co-creators with the universe, aligning their actions with their truest passions and values.

In the climactic moment of their celestial odyssey, Liam and Elysia found themselves at the heart of the Infinite Tapestry—a place where the energies of destiny and purpose merged into a symphony of interconnected threads. They merged with the essence of cosmic design, experiencing a profound union with the infinite possibilities that stretched before them.

Their merging with destiny and purpose awakened a deep sense of empowerment within Liam and Elysia. They embraced their roles as co-creators of their own realities, sharing their expanded wisdom and guiding others on their journeys of self-discovery and purpose. They realized that each individual held a unique thread in the grand tapestry of existence, and that by living authentically and aligning with their true purpose, they contributed to the vibrant fabric of the universe.

The novel concludes with Liam and Elysia continuing their exploration of the Infinite Tapestry, forever inspired by the limitless possibilities and interconnectedness they have discovered. They become catalysts for conscious creation, empowering others to embrace their destinies and co-create a reality where purpose and fulfillment are cherished.

THE INFINITE TAPESTRY: WEAVING THE THREADS OF DESTINY

"The Infinite Tapestry: Weaving the Threads of Destiny" is more than a novel—it is an invitation for readers to embark on their own transformative odyssey, to recognize their innate power as co-creators of their destinies, and to align their actions with their deepest purpose. Through the extraordinary journey of Liam and Elysia, readers are encouraged to explore the realms of destiny and purpose, embrace their unique paths, and co-create a world where each thread in the tapestry of existence shines with purpose and meaning.

As Liam and Elysia continued their exploration of the Infinite Tapestry, they came across a mystical portal that shimmered with an otherworldly glow. Drawn to its magnetic presence, they stepped through the portal and found themselves in a realm that resonated with vibrant energy and divine harmony—a realm known as the Celestial Harmony.

In the Celestial Harmony, the air hummed with a melodic symphony, and celestial lights danced in radiant hues. It was a realm where the harmonious convergence of energies created a sublime equilibrium, and the celestial beings who resided there emanated an aura of profound serenity and balance.

In this sacred realm, they encountered celestial beings known as the Harmonic Guardians. The Harmonic Guardians were embodiments of divine harmony, exuding a sense of peace and unity that transcended earthly realms. They welcomed Liam and Elysia with gentle smiles, inviting them to embrace the power of harmonious coexistence and explore the depths of interconnectedness.

Guided by the Harmonic Guardians, Liam and Elysia embarked on a transformative odyssey through the realms of harmony and unity. They learned to attune their hearts and minds to the subtle rhythms of the universe, to listen to the symphony of existence, and to become conduits of divine harmony.

In their celestial odyssey, they encountered celestial beings who embodied the essence of harmony:

Melodia: A celestial songstress whose voice carried the harmonies of the cosmos. Melodia guided Liam and Elysia in the art of sound and vibration, teaching them to attune to the frequencies of harmony and use their voices as instruments of healing and unity. They learned to weave melodies that dissolved boundaries, uniting hearts and souls in a transcendent experience of oneness.

Equinox: A celestial embodiment of balance and equilibrium. Equinox taught Liam and Elysia the importance of finding balance within themselves and in their interactions with others. They learned to navigate the delicate dance of opposites, embracing the interplay between light and darkness, joy and sorrow, and discovering that true harmony emerged from the integration of seemingly contrasting forces.

Seren: A celestial being who personified the interconnectedness of all life. Seren guided Liam and Elysia to recognize the intrinsic connection between every being in the vast web of existence. They learned to extend compassion and kindness beyond their immediate circles, embracing the understanding that every action rippled through the fabric of the universe, affecting all.

Together, Liam, Elysia, and their celestial companions ventured deeper into the realms of harmony and unity. They participated in sacred rituals, engaged in communal gatherings, and experienced the power of collective intention and shared harmony.

In their celestial odyssey, they discovered that harmony was not a distant ideal, but a lived experience that could be nurtured in every moment. They realized that unity was not the erasure of individuality, but a celebration of the diverse threads that wove the tapestry of existence.

As they deepened their connection with harmony and unity, Liam and Elysia experienced a profound shift in their perception of themselves and the world. They recognized that they were interconnected with all beings and that their choices and actions reverberated through the intricate matrix of existence. They became ambassadors of harmony, weaving threads of unity wherever they went and inspiring others to embrace the power of collective coherence.

In the climactic moment of their celestial odyssey, Liam and Elysia found themselves at the heart of the Celestial Harmony—a place where the energies of harmony and unity merged into a celestial symphony of interconnectedness. They merged with the essence of divine harmony, experiencing a profound union with the infinite chorus that flowed through all of existence.

Their merging with harmony and unity awakened a deep sense of purpose within Liam and Elysia. They became emissaries of peace, sharing their expanded wisdom and guiding others on their journeys toward unity and co-creation. They recognized that every thought, word, and action infused with harmony had the power to create a ripple effect of healing and transformation in the world.

The novel concludes with Liam and Elysia continuing their exploration of the Celestial Harmony, forever inspired by the profound unity and interconnectedness they have discovered. They become catalysts for collective harmony, fostering a global consciousness of peace, cooperation, and love.

THE CELESTIAL HARMONY: EMBRACING THE UNITY OF ALL

"The Celestial Harmony: Embracing the Unity of All" is more than a novel—it is an invitation for readers to embark on their own transformative odyssey, to embrace the power of harmony and interconnectedness, and to co-create a reality where unity and peace prevail. Through the extraordinary journey of Liam and Elysia, readers are encouraged to embrace diversity, nurture compassion, and co-create a world where the symphony of unity resounds in every heart and every corner of existence.

As Liam and Elysia continued their exploration of the Celestial Harmony, they came across a shimmering portal that beckoned them with its radiant glow. Intrigued by its captivating aura, they stepped through the portal and found themselves in a realm that pulsed with vibrant energy—a realm known as the Cosmic Dance.

In the Cosmic Dance, celestial beings swirled in a graceful ballet, their movements synchronized with the rhythm of the cosmos. It was a realm where energy and motion merged into a symphony of divine expression, where the interconnectedness of all things became vividly apparent.

In this sacred realm, they encountered celestial beings known as the Dance Guardians. The Dance Guardians were embodiments of divine movement, radiating an aura of elegance and grace. They welcomed Liam and Elysia with open arms, inviting them to join in the cosmic dance and discover the transformative power of embodied expression.

Guided by the Dance Guardians, Liam and Elysia embarked on a journey of self-discovery and liberation through the realms of movement and expression. They learned to surrender to the flow of energy within their bodies, allowing their movements to become an extension of their souls. They discovered that dance was not just physical, but a profound language that could convey emotions, stories, and connections beyond words.

In their celestial odyssey, they encountered celestial beings who embodied the essence of movement and expression:

Ariadne: A celestial dancer who embodied the art of storytelling through movement. Ariadne guided Liam and Elysia in the exploration of various dance forms, teaching them to express their deepest emotions, dreams, and aspirations through the power of choreography. They learned to use dance as a medium for personal transformation and collective healing.

Rhythmos: A celestial embodiment of rhythm and percussive expression. Rhythmos introduced Liam and Elysia to the world of drumming and percussion, encouraging them to connect with the primal pulse of life. They learned to surrender to the beat, allowing the rhythms to guide their bodies and express their innermost desires and intentions.

Sylph: A celestial being who personified the grace and fluidity of aerial and acrobatic movement. Sylph introduced Liam and Elysia to the world of aerial arts, where they defied gravity and embraced the freedom of flight. They learned to trust their bodies, soar through the air, and connect with the vast expanse of the cosmic dance.

Together, Liam, Elysia, and their celestial companions danced deeper into the realms of movement and expression. They discovered that dance was not limited to a stage or a specific form, but an embodied practice that could be woven into every aspect of life. They learned to find their own unique expressions and create dances that celebrated their individuality and connectedness.

In their celestial odyssey, they discovered that the cosmic dance was not just a metaphor, but a tangible experience of unity and interconnectedness. They realized that every movement they made had an impact, rippling through the fabric of existence and creating a web of collective expression.

As they deepened their connection with movement and expression, Liam and Elysia experienced a profound shift in their perception of themselves and the world. They recognized that their bodies were vessels of divine expression and that through dance, they could access profound states of joy, healing, and transformation. They became conduits of the cosmic dance, inviting others to embrace their own unique movements and co-create a reality where expression was celebrated.

In the climactic moment of their celestial odyssey, Liam and Elysia found themselves at the heart of the Cosmic Dance—a place where the energies of movement and expression merged into a transcendent symphony of interconnected souls. They merged with the essence of the cosmic dance, experiencing a profound union with the infinite flow of divine expression.

Their merging with movement and expression awakened a deep sense of liberation within Liam and Elysia. They became ambassadors of the cosmic dance, sharing their expanded wisdom and guiding others on their journeys of self-discovery and embodied expression. They recognized that the dance had the power to heal, uplift, and unite humanity in a celebration of diverse and interconnected movement.

The novel concludes with Liam and Elysia continuing their exploration of the Cosmic Dance, forever inspired by the transformative power and joy they have discovered. They become catalysts for embodied expression, encouraging others to find their own unique movements and co-create a reality where the dance of life is embraced.

THE COSMIC DANCE: EMBRACING THE RHYTHM OF EXISTENCE

"The Cosmic Dance: Embracing the Rhythm of Existence" is more than a novel—it is an invitation for readers to embark on their own transformative odyssey, to embrace the power of movement and expression, and to co-create a reality where the dance of life is celebrated in all its forms. Through the extraordinary journey of Liam and Elysia, readers are encouraged to unleash their inner movements, explore the depths of expression, and co-create a world where the cosmic dance resounds in every heart and every step.

As Liam and Elysia continued their exploration of the Cosmic Dance, they came upon a hidden grove nestled deep within the realm. The grove emanated a vibrant energy, drawing them closer with its enchanting allure. They entered the grove and found themselves surrounded by majestic trees, their branches swaying in harmony with the celestial rhythms.

In the heart of the grove, they discovered a sacred circle—a space infused with ancient wisdom and mystical energy. Intrigued by its power, they stepped into the circle and felt a surge of connection to the cosmic forces that flowed through the universe. It was a place of profound communion with the elements and the celestial beings that presided over them.

In this sacred space, they encountered celestial beings known as the Elemental Guardians. The Elemental Guardians were embodiments of the primal forces of nature, each representing a specific element—earth, air, fire, and water. They welcomed Liam and Elysia with serene smiles, inviting them to attune to the energies of the elements and discover their profound connection to the natural world.

Guided by the Elemental Guardians, Liam and Elysia embarked on a transformative journey through the realms of nature and elemental magic. They learned to commune with the elements, harness their energies, and co-create with the forces that shaped the world around them. They discovered that by aligning themselves with the elemental energies, they could access ancient wisdom and unlock their own innate abilities.

In their celestial odyssey, they encountered celestial beings who embodied the essence of the elements:

Gaia: A celestial embodiment of the Earth element. Gaia guided Liam and Elysia to connect with the grounding and nurturing energy of the Earth. They learned to cultivate a deep sense of rootedness, honor the natural world, and embrace the cycles of life and growth.

Zephyr: A celestial embodiment of the Air element. Zephyr taught Liam and Elysia to attune to the gentle currents of the wind and the invisible forces that moved through the air. They learned to cultivate clarity of thought, embrace change, and harness the power of breath and intention.

Pyra: A celestial embodiment of the Fire element. Pyra kindled the flame of passion and transformation within Liam and Elysia. They learned to harness the transformative power of fire, cultivate inner strength, and ignite their creative and spiritual endeavors.

Aqua: A celestial embodiment of the Water element. Aqua guided Liam and Elysia to embrace the fluidity and emotional depth of water. They learned to connect with their intuition, navigate the currents of their emotions, and honor the healing and purifying qualities of water.

Together, Liam, Elysia, and their celestial companions delved deeper into the realms of nature and elemental magic. They immersed themselves in the beauty of the natural world, communed with the spirits of plants and animals, and co-created with the elements to bring about harmony and transformation.

In their celestial odyssey, they discovered that the elements were not separate entities but interconnected aspects of a greater whole. They realized that by embracing their connection to nature and the elements, they could tap into the inherent wisdom of the universe and access profound states of harmony and balance.

As they deepened their connection with nature and the elements, Liam and Elysia experienced a profound shift in their perception of themselves and the world. They recognized that they were interconnected with all of creation, and their actions had the power to bring about healing and restoration. They became stewards of the natural world, nurturing a deep reverence for the Earth and embracing their roles as guardians of its well-being.

In the climactic moment of their celestial odyssey, Liam and Elysia found themselves at the center of the sacred circle, surrounded by the Elemental Guardians—a place where the energies of nature and elemental magic merged into a symphony of interconnected forces. They merged with the essence of the elements, experiencing a profound union with the infinite power that flowed through all of existence.

Their merging with nature and the elements awakened a deep sense of harmony within Liam and Elysia. They became emissaries of the natural world, sharing their expanded wisdom and guiding others on their journeys of connection and co-creation with the elements. They recognized that the balance and harmony found in nature were reflections of the balance and harmony that could be cultivated within every individual and society.

The novel concludes with Liam and Elysia continuing their exploration of the Cosmic Dance, forever inspired by the profound connection and reverence they have discovered for nature and the elements. They become catalysts for ecological stewardship and co-creation, fostering a global consciousness that honors the interdependence of all living beings.

THE ELEMENTAL SYMPHONY: EMBRACING THE HARMONY OF NATURE

"The Elemental Symphony: Embracing the Harmony of Nature" is more than a novel—it is an invitation for readers to embark on their own transformative odyssey, to deepen their connection with nature and the elements, and to co-create a reality where humanity lives in harmony with the natural world. Through the extraordinary journey of Liam and Elysia, readers are encouraged to rediscover their inherent bond with the Earth, embrace nature stared.

As Liam and Elysia continued their exploration of the Cosmic Dance, they felt a magnetic pull toward a radiant celestial temple nestled within the realm. Its majestic presence beckoned them closer, promising profound revelations and spiritual growth. Intrigued and filled with anticipation, they approached the temple, its shimmering doors opening to welcome them inside.

The interior of the celestial temple was bathed in a soft, ethereal light, casting a serene glow upon everything within. They found themselves in a space adorned with ancient symbols, sacred artifacts, and shelves lined with mystical tomes. It was a place of timeless wisdom and spiritual awakening—an oasis of enlightenment within the Cosmic Dance.

In this sacred space, they encountered celestial beings known as the Keepers of Knowledge. The Keepers were embodiments of divine wisdom, emanating an aura of profound insight and illumination. They greeted Liam and Elysia with gentle smiles, inviting them to delve into the depths of spiritual exploration and unlock the secrets of the universe.

Guided by the Keepers of Knowledge, Liam and Elysia embarked on a transformative journey of spiritual awakening and self-discovery. They learned to open their hearts and minds to the mysteries of existence, to embrace their connection to the divine, and to tap into their inner wisdom.

In their celestial odyssey, they encountered celestial beings who embodied the essence of spiritual awakening:

Sophia: A celestial sage who radiated the wisdom of the ages. Sophia guided Liam and Elysia in the exploration of ancient teachings, esoteric knowledge, and metaphysical principles. They learned to cultivate inner stillness, expand their consciousness, and integrate divine wisdom into their daily lives.

Ananda: A celestial mystic who embodied the experience of divine bliss and unconditional love. Ananda introduced Liam and Elysia to the transformative power of heart-centered living, guiding them to cultivate compassion, gratitude, and deep connection to the Source. They learned to align with the frequency of love and allow it to guide their every interaction and decision.

Metatron: A celestial archangel who held the keys to cosmic harmony and divine order. Metatron helped Liam and Elysia attune to the sacred geometry of the universe, understanding the underlying patterns and symmetries that governed all of creation. They learned to work with energetic grids, activate their own light bodies, and embody the harmony and balance of the cosmos.

Together, Liam, Elysia, and their celestial companions delved deeper into the realms of spiritual awakening and divine wisdom. They explored meditation, energy healing, and various spiritual practices, integrating the teachings into their everyday lives. They discovered that the path of spiritual growth was not separate from the dance of existence, but an intrinsic part of it.

In their celestial odyssey, they discovered that spiritual awakening was a journey of remembrance—a reconnection with their true essence and the divine spark within. They realized that the answers they sought were not external but resided within their own hearts and souls. They became vessels of divine wisdom, sharing their expanded consciousness and guiding others on their journeys of spiritual exploration.

As they deepened their connection with spiritual awakening, Liam and Elysia experienced a profound shift in their perception of themselves and the world. They recognized that they were not separate from the divine, but integral parts of the cosmic tapestry. They became beacons of light, radiating love, wisdom, and compassion in all they did.

In the climactic moment of their celestial odyssey, Liam and Elysia found themselves at the heart of the celestial temple—a place where the energies of spiritual awakening merged into a symphony of transcendent illumination. They merged with the essence of divine knowledge, experiencing a profound union with the infinite wisdom that flowed through all of existence.

Their merging with spiritual awakening awakened a deep sense of purpose within Liam and Elysia. They became messengers of divine wisdom, sharing their expanded consciousness and guiding others on their journeys of spiritual exploration. They recognized that true enlightenment was not an endpoint, but an ever-evolving process of growth and self-discovery.

The novel concludes with Liam and Elysia continuing their exploration of the Cosmic Dance, forever inspired by the profound spiritual insights and connections they have discovered. They become catalysts for spiritual awakening and transformation, fostering a global consciousness of love, wisdom, and unity.

As Liam and Elysia continued their exploration of the Cosmic Dance, they felt a magnetic pull toward a radiant celestial temple nestled within the realm. Its majestic presence beckoned them closer, promising profound revelations and spiritual growth. Intrigued and filled with anticipation, they approached the temple, its shimmering doors opening to welcome them inside.

The interior of the celestial temple was bathed in a soft, ethereal light, casting a serene glow upon everything within. They found themselves in a space adorned with ancient symbols, sacred artifacts, and shelves lined with mystical tomes. It was a place of timeless wisdom and spiritual awakening—an oasis of enlightenment within the Cosmic Dance.

In this sacred space, they encountered celestial beings known as the Keepers of Knowledge. The Keepers were embodiments of divine wisdom, emanating an aura of profound insight and illumination. They greeted Liam and Elysia with gentle smiles, inviting them to delve into the depths of spiritual exploration and unlock the secrets of the universe.

Guided by the Keepers of Knowledge, Liam and Elysia embarked on a transformative journey of spiritual awakening and self-discovery. They learned to open their hearts and minds to the mysteries of existence, to embrace their connection to the divine, and to tap into their inner wisdom.

In their celestial odyssey, they encountered celestial beings who embodied the essence of spiritual awakening:

Sophia: A celestial sage who radiated the wisdom of the ages. Sophia guided Liam and Elysia in the exploration of ancient teachings, esoteric knowledge, and metaphysical principles. They learned to cultivate inner stillness, expand their consciousness, and integrate divine wisdom into their daily lives.

Ananda: A celestial mystic who embodied the experience of divine bliss and unconditional love. Ananda introduced Liam and Elysia to the transformative power of heart-centered living, guiding them to cultivate compassion, gratitude, and deep connection to the Source. They learned to align with the frequency of love and allow it to guide their every interaction and decision.

Metatron: A celestial archangel who held the keys to cosmic harmony and divine order. Metatron helped Liam and Elysia attune to the sacred geometry of the universe, understanding the underlying patterns and symmetries that governed all of creation. They learned to work with energetic grids, activate their own light bodies, and embody the harmony and balance of the cosmos.

Luna: A celestial being who personified the cycles of the moon and the intuitive wisdom it represented. Luna guided Liam and Elysia to connect with their inner knowing, to trust their intuition, and to embrace the ebb and flow of life. They learned to honor the cycles of creation, release, and renewal, and to align with the guidance of their inner guidance.

Together, Liam, Elysia, and their celestial companions delved deeper into the realms of spiritual awakening and divine wisdom. They explored meditation, energy healing, and various spiritual practices, integrating the teachings into their everyday lives. They discovered that the path of spiritual growth was not separate from the dance of existence, but an intrinsic part of it.

In their celestial odyssey, they discovered that spiritual awakening was a journey of remembrance—a reconnection with their true essence and the divine spark within. They realized that the answers they sought were not external but resided within their own hearts and souls. They became vessels of divine wisdom, sharing their expanded consciousness and guiding others on their journeys of spiritual exploration.

As they deepened their connection with spiritual awakening, Liam and Elysia experienced a profound shift in their perception of themselves and the world. They recognized that they were not separate from the divine, but integral parts of the cosmic tapestry. They became beacons of light, radiating love, wisdom, and compassion in all they did.

In the climactic moment of their celestial odyssey, Liam and Elysia found themselves at the heart of the celestial temple—a place where the energies of spiritual awakening merged into a symphony of transcendent illumination. They merged with the essence of divine knowledge, experiencing a profound union with the infinite wisdom that flowed through all of existence.

Their merging with spiritual awakening awakened a deep sense of purpose within Liam and Elysia. They became messengers of divine wisdom, sharing their expanded consciousness and guiding others on their journeys of spiritual exploration. They recognized that true enlightenment was not an endpoint, but an ever-evolving process of growth and self-discovery.

The novel concludes with Liam and Elysia continuing their exploration of the Cosmic Dance, forever inspired by the profound spiritual insights and connections they have discovered. They become catalysts for spiritual awakening and transformation, fostering a global consciousness of love, wisdom, and unity.

THE CELESTIAL AWAKENING: EMBARKING ON THE PATH OF ILLUMINATION

"The Celestial Awakening: Embarking on the Path of Illumination" is more than a novel—it is an invitation for readers to embark on their own transformative odyssey, to embrace the power of spiritual awakening, and to co-create a reality where humanity lives in alignment with divine wisdom. Through the extraordinary journey of Liam and Elysia, readers are encouraged to seek the truth within, expand their consciousness, and navigate the dance of existence with divine guidance.

"The Celestial Awakening: Embarking on the Path of Illumination" is more than a novel—it is an invitation for readers to embark on their own transformative odyssey, to embrace the power of spiritual awakening, and to co-create a reality where humanity lives in alignment with divine wisdom. Through the extraordinary journey of Liam and Elysia, readers are encouraged to seek the truth within, expand their consciousness, and navigate the dance of existence with divine guidance.

As Liam and Elysia continued their exploration of the Cosmic Dance, they were drawn deeper into the mystical realm by an irresistible pull. They followed the ethereal glow that led them to a sacred waterfall, cascading with shimmering waters that sparkled like liquid stardust. Mesmerized by its beauty, they approached the waterfall, feeling a sense of awe and reverence for the magic that permeated the air.

As they stepped into the gentle mist of the waterfall, a pathway materialized, guiding them to a hidden realm known as the Veil of Whispers. It was a place where the boundary between the physical world and the ethereal realms became blurred, and the wisdom of the unseen was whispered on the breeze.

In this enchanted realm, they encountered celestial beings known as the Whisperers. The Whisperers were embodiments of ethereal wisdom, their voices carrying the secrets of the universe. They greeted Liam and Elysia with serene smiles, inviting them to attune to the whispers of the Veil and discover the profound knowledge that lay beyond the ordinary senses.

Guided by the Whisperers, Liam and Elysia embarked on a transformative journey through the realms of intuition and spiritual insight. They learned to quiet their minds, trust their inner guidance, and embrace the subtle nudges of the universe. They discovered that the whispers of the Veil held profound messages and synchronicities that guided them on their path.

In their celestial odyssey, they encountered celestial beings who embodied the essence of intuitive wisdom:

Orion: A celestial seer who possessed the gift of foresight and divination. Orion guided Liam and Elysia in the exploration of prophecy, dreams, and the signs that revealed hidden truths. They learned to interpret the symbols of the universe, trust their intuitive visions, and discern the deeper meanings behind the veiled messages.

Seraphine: A celestial empath who embodied deep sensitivity and emotional intuition. Seraphine introduced Liam and Elysia to the realm of emotions and energetic vibrations. They learned to attune to their own emotions, embrace empathy, and navigate the intricate web of energy that connected all beings.

Astral: A celestial being who personified the exploration of astral projection and the subtle realms beyond the physical. Astral guided Liam and Elysia to venture beyond the confines of the physical body, exploring the astral planes and communing with celestial entities. They learned to navigate the realms of energy and consciousness, expanding their awareness beyond the material world.

Together, Liam, Elysia, and their celestial companions delved deeper into the realms of intuition and spiritual insight. They honed their intuitive abilities, cultivated deep listening, and embraced the interconnectedness of all things. They discovered that the whispers of the Veil were not limited to ethereal realms but could be found within every breath and moment of life.

In their celestial odyssey, they discovered that intuitive wisdom was not a gift reserved for a chosen few, but an inherent part of their being. They realized that they were conduits of divine guidance, and by trusting their intuition, they could navigate the dance of life with grace and clarity. They became instruments of the cosmic symphony, following the harmonious melodies of the universe.

As they deepened their connection with intuition and spiritual insight, Liam and Elysia experienced a profound shift in their perception of themselves and the world. They recognized that they were connected to a vast web of knowledge and guidance, and their inner wisdom held the keys to their true potential. They became beacons of intuitive wisdom, radiating light and clarity in all they did.

In the climactic moment of their celestial odyssey, Liam and Elysia found themselves at the heart of the Veil of Whispers—a place where the energies of intuition and spiritual insight merged into a symphony of ethereal whispers. They merged with the essence of intuitive wisdom, experiencing a profound union with the infinite knowledge that flowed through all of existence.

Their merging with intuition and spiritual insight awakened a deep sense of purpose within Liam and Elysia. They became messengers of the Veil, sharing their expanded consciousness and guiding others on their journeys of inner knowing. They recognized that true wisdom resided not only in external knowledge but in the depths of their own being.

The novel concludes with Liam and Elysia continuing their exploration of the Cosmic Dance, forever inspired by the profound intuitive wisdom and connections they have discovered. They become catalysts for inner knowing and transformation, fostering a global consciousness that honors the power of intuition and the whispers of the universe.

THE VEIL OF WHISPERS: EMBRACING THE INTUITIVE PATH

"The Veil of Whispers: Embracing the Intuitive Path" is more than a novel—it is an invitation for readers to embark on their own transformative odyssey, to embrace the power of intuition, and to co-create a reality where humanity lives in alignment with the whispers of the universe. Through the extraordinary journey of Liam and Elysia, readers are encouraged to listen to the whispers of their hearts, trust their inner guidance, and dance with the mystical energies that guide their path.

As Liam and Elysia continued their exploration of the Cosmic Dance, they felt a magnetic pull toward a hidden realm shrouded in mist. Intrigued by its mysterious allure, they followed their intuition and embarked on a path that led them deep into the realm of Shadowsong. This ethereal realm resonated with a haunting melody that echoed through the air, captivating their senses.

In the realm of Shadowsong, they encountered celestial beings known as the Songweavers. The Songweavers were embodiments of ethereal melodies, their voices carrying the essence of emotions and experiences. They greeted Liam and Elysia with enchanting harmonies, inviting them to unravel the tapestry of emotions and discover the transformative power of music and song.

Guided by the Songweavers, Liam and Elysia embarked on a journey of emotional exploration and self-expression through the language of music.

They learned to attune their hearts to the vibrations of sound, to channel their emotions into melodies, and to unleash the power of music to heal, uplift, and connect with others.

In their celestial odyssey, they encountered celestial beings who embodied the essence of music and song:

Melora: A celestial singer who radiated the purity and resonance of the human voice. Melora guided Liam and Elysia in the exploration of vocal expression, teaching them to embrace the power of their own voices and use singing as a means of emotional release and soulful connection.

Harmon: A celestial instrumentalist who personified the transformative power of musical instruments. Harmon introduced Liam and Elysia to a myriad of instruments, each carrying its unique voice and ability to evoke emotions. They learned to play instruments, compose melodies, and express their innermost feelings through the universal language of music.

Serenade: A celestial conductor who embodied the art of orchestration and collaboration. Serenade guided Liam and Elysia in the creation of harmonious musical ensembles, teaching them to synchronize their energies, blend their voices, and co-create symphonies of unity and beauty. They learned the importance of harmony, collaboration, and the profound impact of collective expression.

Together, Liam, Elysia, and their celestial companions delved deeper into the realms of music and song. They explored different genres, experimented with improvisation, and infused their compositions with the emotions and experiences that stirred within them. They discovered that music had the power to transcend language, cultural barriers, and time, reaching deep into the souls of others.

In their celestial odyssey, they discovered that music was not just an art form, but a profound tool for healing and transformation. They realized that through music, they could touch the hearts of others, ignite inspiration, and create a ripple effect of positive change. They became conduits of emotional expression, using their melodies to convey stories, evoke emotions, and unite hearts.

As they deepened their connection with music and song, Liam and Elysia experienced a profound shift in their perception of themselves and the world. They recognized that their voices and melodies held the power to heal, to uplift, and to bring people together. They became catalysts for harmony and unity, using their music to bridge divides and awaken the inherent connectedness of all beings.

In the climactic moment of their celestial odyssey, Liam and Elysia found themselves at the heart of Shadowsong—a place where the energies of music and song merged into a symphony of emotional resonance. They merged with the essence of music, experiencing a profound union with the infinite power that flowed through all of existence.

Their merging with music and song awakened a deep sense of purpose within Liam and Elysia. They became messengers of the melody, sharing their expanded wisdom and guiding others on their journeys of emotional exploration and self-expression. They recognized that true beauty resided not only in the notes themselves but in the emotional landscapes they evoked.

The novel concludes with Liam and Elysia continuing their exploration of the Cosmic Dance, forever inspired by the profound emotional connections and transformative power they have discovered through music and song. They become ambassadors of the Songweavers, fostering a global consciousness that honors the healing and unifying power of music.

THE MELODIES OF THE SOUL: WEAVING THE TAPESTRY OF EMOTION

"The Melodies of the Soul: Weaving the Tapestry of Emotion" is more than a novel—it is an invitation for readers to embark on their own transformative odyssey, to embrace the power of music and song, and to co-create a reality where humanity expresses and connects through the melodies of the soul. Through the extraordinary journey of Liam and Elysia, readers are encouraged to unlock their own emotional landscapes, embrace the transformative power of music, and dance to the rhythm of their own unique song.

As Liam and Elysia continued their exploration of the Cosmic Dance, they discovered a hidden path that led them to a mystical realm known as the Luminous Garden. This ethereal sanctuary was filled with radiant flowers that emitted a soft, iridescent glow, casting enchanting colors upon everything around them. The air was perfumed with the delicate fragrance of blossoms, and the atmosphere was charged with a sense of pure magic.

In the heart of the Luminous Garden, they encountered celestial beings known as the Lightweavers. The Lightweavers were embodiments of ethereal light, radiating warmth, love, and healing energy. They greeted Liam and Elysia with gentle smiles, inviting them to immerse themselves in the luminous energies and discover the transformative power of light and healing.

Guided by the Lightweavers, Liam and Elysia embarked on a journey of healing and self-discovery. They learned to attune their hearts to the healing frequencies of light, to embrace the power of energy healing, and to channel divine light for their own well-being and the well-being of others. They discovered that light was not just an external force, but an inherent part of their own essence.

In their celestial odyssey, they encountered celestial beings who embodied the essence of light and healing:

Aurora: A celestial healer who radiated the divine light of compassion and transformation. Aurora guided Liam and Elysia in the exploration of energy healing modalities, teaching them to balance and restore the flow of energy within their bodies and to facilitate healing in others. They learned to harness the healing power of light, release energetic blockages, and activate their own innate healing abilities.

Solara: A celestial guardian of the sun, embodying the illuminating and life-giving qualities of solar energy. Solara introduced Liam and Elysia to the transformative power of the sun, teaching them to absorb its radiant energy, nurture their bodies with light, and embrace the vitality and joy that came from aligning with the solar frequencies. They learned to harness the sun's energy for healing, rejuvenation, and spiritual growth.

Lumina: A celestial guide who personified the spiritual light and inner illumination. Lumina guided Liam and Elysia in the exploration of their own inner light, teaching them to cultivate inner peace, clarity, and spiritual connection. They learned to expand their consciousness, embrace their divine essence, and shine their light in the world, inspiring others to do the same.

Together, Liam, Elysia, and their celestial companions delved deeper into the realms of light and healing. They practiced various energy healing techniques, connected with the luminous energies of the Luminous Garden, and discovered the profound transformative power of light. They realized that healing was not just a physical process but a holistic journey that encompassed mind, body, and spirit.

In their celestial odyssey, they discovered that the power of healing was not limited to their own well-being but extended to the healing of the collective and the planet itself. They recognized that by embracing their own healing journey, they could become catalysts for global healing and transformation. They became conduits of divine light, spreading love, compassion, and healing wherever they went.

As they deepened their connection with light and healing, Liam and Elysia experienced a profound shift in their perception of themselves and the world. They recognized that they were not just individuals but interconnected beings, and their own healing journey had the power to uplift and inspire others. They became agents of transformation, using their light and healing abilities to bring about positive change in the world.

In the climactic moment of their celestial odyssey, Liam and Elysia found themselves at the center of the Luminous Garden—a place where the energies of light and healing merged into a symphony of divine radiance. They merged with the essence of light, experiencing a profound union with the infinite healing power that flowed through all of existence.

Their merging with light and healing awakened a deep sense of purpose within Liam and Elysia. They became messengers of divine light, sharing their expanded wisdom and guiding others on their journeys of healing and self-discovery. They recognized that true healing was not just the absence of physical ailments but a harmonious integration of mind, body, and spirit.

The novel concludes with Liam and Elysia continuing their exploration of the Cosmic Dance, forever inspired by the profound healing connections and transformative power they have discovered through light and healing. They become beacons of light and agents of healing, fostering a global consciousness that honors the interconnectedness of all beings and embraces the power of divine light.

THE LUMINOUS PATH: EMBRACING THE HEALING JOURNEY

"The Luminous Path: Embracing the Healing Journey" is more than a novel—it is an invitation for readers to embark on their own transformative odyssey, to embrace the power of light and healing, and to co-create a reality where humanity thrives in well-being and wholeness. Through the extraordinary journey of Liam and Elysia, readers are encouraged to awaken their own inner light, embrace the transformative power of healing, and illuminate the world with love and compassion.

As Liam and Elysia continued their exploration of the Cosmic Dance, they felt a magnetic pull toward a hidden realm pulsating with vibrant energy. They followed their instincts and embarked on a path that led them to the realm of Etheria. It was a realm where the boundaries between the physical and spiritual realms dissolved, and the raw essence of creation danced freely.

In the realm of Etheria, they encountered celestial beings known as the Essence Weavers. The Essence Weavers were embodiments of divine creation, radiating the pure energy that formed the building blocks of the universe. They greeted Liam and Elysia with warm smiles, inviting them to tap into the creative forces within and explore the boundless possibilities of manifestation.

Guided by the Essence Weavers, Liam and Elysia embarked on a journey of creation and co-creation. They learned to harness the power of intention, visualization, and energetic alignment to manifest their desires and shape their reality. They discovered that they were co-creators in the dance of existence, able to shape their lives through their thoughts, emotions, and actions.

In their celestial odyssey, they encountered celestial beings who embodied the essence of creation and co-creation:

Aria: A celestial muse who embodied the essence of inspiration and artistic expression. Aria guided Liam and Elysia in the exploration of their creative potentials, teaching them to tap into the wellspring of inspiration that resided within. They learned to express their unique creative voices, whether through art, music, writing, or any other form of creative expression.

Atlas: A celestial architect who personified the art of manifestation and building realities. Atlas introduced Liam and Elysia to the principles of manifestation, teaching them to clarify their intentions, align with their desires, and take inspired action to bring their visions into fruition. They learned to navigate the subtle energies of manifestation and create harmonious and abundant realities.

Althea: A celestial healer who embodied the transformative power of love and compassion in co-creation. Althea guided Liam and Elysia in the exploration of heart-centered manifestation, teaching them to infuse their intentions and creations with love, compassion, and the highest good of all. They learned to align their desires with the greater collective consciousness, contributing to the well-being and upliftment of humanity.

Together, Liam, Elysia, and their celestial companions delved deeper into the realms of creation and co-creation. They cultivated their creative energies, visualized their dreams and desires, and took inspired action to manifest their visions. They discovered that the act of creation was not just about achieving personal goals but about aligning with their highest purpose and contributing to the greater good.

In their celestial odyssey, they discovered that creation and co-creation were not limited to tangible outcomes but also included the creation of experiences, relationships, and a life infused with meaning and fulfillment. They realized that their thoughts, emotions, and intentions had a profound impact on the world around them, shaping their reality in ways they had never imagined.

As they deepened their connection with creation and co-creation, Liam and Elysia experienced a profound shift in their perception of themselves and the world. They recognized that they were not passive observers but active participants in the grand symphony of creation. They became conscious creators, using their intentions and actions to shape a reality that aligned with their deepest values and desires.

In the climactic moment of their celestial odyssey, Liam and Elysia found themselves at the heart of Etheria—a place where the energies of creation and co-creation merged into a symphony of infinite possibilities. They merged with the essence of creation, experiencing a profound union with the limitless creative potential that flowed through all of existence.

Their merging with creation and co-creation awakened a deep sense of purpose within Liam and Elysia. They became master co-creators, sharing their expanded wisdom and guiding others on their journeys of conscious manifestation. They recognized that true fulfillment came from aligning their creations with their soul's purpose and contributing to the evolution of consciousness.

The novel concludes with Liam and Elysia continuing their exploration of the Cosmic Dance, forever inspired by the profound connections and transformative power they have discovered through creation and co-creation. They become agents of conscious manifestation, fostering a global consciousness that honors the creative potential within each individual and co-creates a reality grounded in love, harmony, and abundance.

THE ESSENCE OF CREATION: AWAKENING THE POWER WITHIN

"The Essence of Creation: Awakening the Power Within" is more than a novel—it is an invitation for readers to embark on their own transformative odyssey, to embrace the power of creation and co-creation, and to co-create a reality where humanity thrives in alignment with their highest visions and aspirations. Through the extraordinary journey of Liam and Elysia, readers are encouraged to unleash their creative potential, align their creations with their soul's purpose, and dance with the universe as conscious co-creators.

As Liam and Elysia continued their exploration of the Cosmic Dance, they were drawn toward a hidden realm shimmering with crystalline light. The realm called Crystalia resonated with the essence of clarity, purity, and inner illumination. Intrigued by its ethereal beauty, they followed the radiant path that led them deeper into the crystalline realm.

In Crystalia, they encountered celestial beings known as the Crystal Guardians. The Crystal Guardians were embodiments of the wisdom and energy held within the crystalline structures that adorned the realm. They greeted Liam and Elysia with sparkling eyes, inviting them to explore the transformative power of crystals and tap into their inherent energies for healing, guidance, and spiritual growth.

Guided by the Crystal Guardians, Liam and Elysia embarked on a journey of crystal consciousness and awakening. They learned to attune their energy to the vibrational frequencies of crystals, to harness their unique properties, and to embrace their transformative energies. They discovered that crystals were not merely beautiful objects but potent tools for inner alchemy and self-realization.

In their celestial odyssey, they encountered celestial beings who embodied the essence of crystals and their energies:

Amethysta: A celestial seer who radiated the wisdom and intuition of amethyst crystals. Amethysta guided Liam and Elysia in the exploration of their own intuitive abilities, teaching them to awaken their third eye and connect with higher realms of knowledge and insight. They learned to use amethyst crystals to enhance their intuition, deepen their spiritual connection, and access higher realms of consciousness.

Rose Quartzia: A celestial healer who personified the unconditional love and compassion of rose quartz crystals. Rose Quartzia introduced Liam and Elysia to the transformative power of love and self-care. They learned to use rose quartz crystals to heal emotional wounds, open their hearts to love, and cultivate a deeper sense of self-acceptance and compassion.

Citrinus: A celestial manifestor who embodied the abundance and manifestation energies of citrine crystals. Citrinus guided Liam and Elysia in the exploration of their own manifesting abilities, teaching them to align their energy with the frequency of abundance, prosperity, and success. They learned to use citrine crystals to amplify their intentions, attract positive opportunities, and manifest their desires.

Selenitea: A celestial purifier who personified the cleansing and clearing energies of selenite crystals. Selenitea introduced Liam and Elysia to the power of energetic purification and spiritual upliftment. They learned to use selenite crystals to cleanse their energy field, release stagnant emotions, and create a harmonious environment for spiritual growth and transformation.

Together, Liam, Elysia, and their celestial companions delved deeper into the realms of crystal consciousness. They explored different types of crystals, learned their unique properties, and integrated their energies into their daily lives. They discovered that crystals were powerful allies in their spiritual journey, supporting them in healing, guidance, and energetic alignment.

In their celestial odyssey, they discovered that crystals were not mere external tools but reflections of the crystalline energy within themselves. They realized that their own beings were composed of intricate energetic structures and that they had the power to cultivate their inner crystalline light. They became harmonizers of energy, using the wisdom of crystals to bring balance, clarity, and transformation to themselves and the world around them.

As they deepened their connection with crystal consciousness, Liam and Elysia experienced a profound shift in their perception of themselves and the world. They recognized that they were not separate from the Earth and the cosmos but interconnected with the energies that flowed through them. They became guardians of the Earth's crystalline energy, honoring and preserving the wisdom held within the mineral kingdom.

In the climactic moment of their celestial odyssey, Liam and Elysia found themselves at the heart of Crystalia—a place where the energies of crystals and their consciousness merged into a symphony of luminous radiance. They merged with the essence of crystal consciousness, experiencing a profound union with the infinite wisdom and transformative power that flowed through all of existence.

Their merging with crystal consciousness awakened a deep sense of purpose within Liam and Elysia. They became emissaries of the crystal kingdom, sharing their expanded wisdom and guiding others on their journeys of crystal consciousness and self-realization. They recognized that true healing and transformation were not external pursuits but journeys of inner alchemy and alignment with the crystalline light within.

The novel concludes with Liam and Elysia continuing their exploration of the Cosmic Dance, forever inspired by the profound connections and transformative power they have discovered through crystal consciousness. They become stewards of the crystal kingdom, fostering a global consciousness that honors the wisdom and energy held within the mineral realm.

CRYSTALLINE AWAKENING: EMBRACING THE WISDOM WITHIN

"Crystalline Awakening: Embracing the Wisdom Within" is more than a novel—it is an invitation for readers to embark on their own transformative odyssey, to embrace the power of crystal consciousness, and to co-create a reality where humanity harmonizes with the crystalline energy of the Earth. Through the extraordinary journey of Liam and Elysia, readers are encouraged to awaken their own crystalline light, honor the wisdom of the crystal kingdom, and dance with the energies that ignite their inner illumination.

As Liam and Elysia continued their exploration of the Cosmic Dance, they found themselves drawn to a hidden realm of ancient wisdom and mystical enchantment. This realm, known as Mystoria, was veiled in a shimmering mist that seemed to hold the secrets of the universe. Intrigued by its allure, they followed a path that led them deeper into the heart of Mystoria.

In Mystoria, they encountered celestial beings known as the Sagekeepers. The Sagekeepers were embodiments of ancient wisdom and profound insight, their eyes sparkling with knowledge passed down through the ages. They greeted Liam and Elysia with a knowing smile, inviting them to immerse themselves in the mysteries of the realm and discover the transformative power of wisdom and enlightenment.

Guided by the Sagekeepers, Liam and Elysia embarked on a journey of inner exploration and self-discovery. They delved into the depths of their souls, seeking to unlock the ancient wisdom that lay dormant within. They learned to quiet their minds, listen to the whispers of their hearts, and connect with the eternal truths that resonated in the realm of Mystoria.

In their celestial odyssey, they encountered celestial beings who embodied the essence of wisdom and enlightenment:

Sophia: A celestial philosopher who radiated the wisdom and intellectual depth of the ancient sages. Sophia guided Liam and Elysia in the exploration of philosophy, critical thinking, and the pursuit of knowledge. They learned to question the nature of reality, ponder the mysteries of existence, and expand their understanding of the world.

Avalon: A celestial mystic who personified the spiritual insights and intuitive knowing of the ancient seers. Avalon introduced Liam and Elysia to the realm of mysticism, teaching them to tap into their intuition, explore the unseen realms, and connect with the divine essence that permeated all of creation. They learned to trust their inner guidance, access higher states of consciousness, and embrace the mystical path.

Orionis: A celestial storyteller who embodied the power of ancient myths and legends. Orionis guided Liam and Elysia in the exploration of storytelling, symbolism, and the archetypal patterns that echoed through time. They learned to unravel the hidden meanings behind stories, connect with their own unique narratives, and find wisdom and inspiration in the tales of old.

Together, Liam, Elysia, and their celestial companions delved deeper into the realms of wisdom and enlightenment. They engaged in deep philosophical discussions, contemplated the mysteries of existence, and embraced the transformative power of inner illumination. They discovered that wisdom was not confined to scholarly pursuits but permeated every aspect of life, guiding their choices, relationships, and spiritual growth.

In their celestial odyssey, they discovered that wisdom and enlightenment were not destinations to be reached but ongoing journeys of self-discovery and personal growth. They realized that true wisdom resided not just in external knowledge but in the depths of their own being. They became seekers of truth, open to the continuous unfoldment of wisdom that life offered.

As they deepened their connection with wisdom and enlightenment, Liam and Elysia experienced a profound shift in their perception of themselves and the world. They recognized that they were not separate from the wisdom of the ages but were vessels through which ancient truths could be expressed and embodied. They became beacons of wisdom, sharing their expanded understanding and guiding others on their own paths of self-discovery.

In the climactic moment of their celestial odyssey, Liam and Elysia found themselves at the heart of Mystoria—a place where the energies of wisdom and enlightenment merged into a symphony of ancient knowing. They merged with the essence of wisdom, experiencing a profound union with the eternal truths that flowed through all of existence.

Their merging with wisdom and enlightenment awakened a deep sense of purpose within Liam and Elysia. They became messengers of ancient wisdom, sharing their expanded insights and guiding others on their journeys of self-discovery and enlightenment. They recognized that true enlightenment was not an isolated state but a collective awakening that uplifted the consciousness of humanity.

The novel concludes with Liam and Elysia continuing their exploration of the Cosmic Dance, forever inspired by the profound connections and transformative power they have discovered through wisdom and enlightenment. They become ambassadors of ancient wisdom, fostering a global consciousness that honors the wisdom of the past, embraces the present moment, and co-creates a future guided by enlightened awareness.

MYSTORIA: UNVEILING THE PATH OF WISDOM

"Mystoria: Unveiling the Path of Wisdom" is more than a novel—it is an invitation for readers to embark on their own transformative odyssey, to embrace the power of wisdom and enlightenment, and to dance with the eternal truths that reside within. Through the extraordinary journey of Liam and Elysia, readers are encouraged to unlock their own inner wisdom, seek truth, and embrace the profound insights that illuminate the path of self-discovery.

As Liam and Elysia continued their exploration of the Cosmic Dance, they found themselves drawn towards a mysterious realm that exuded an ethereal glow. The realm, known as Lumina, shimmered with radiant light that seemed to emanate from within every living being that resided there. Intrigued by its captivating beauty, they followed a path that led them deeper into the heart of Lumina.

In Lumina, they encountered celestial beings known as the Lightseekers. The Lightseekers were embodiments of divine illumination and spiritual awakening, radiating a profound sense of inner peace and joy. They greeted Liam and Elysia with gentle smiles, inviting them to embrace the transformative power of light and discover the true nature of their own divine essence.

Guided by the Lightseekers, Liam and Elysia embarked on a journey of inner illumination and spiritual growth. They learned to attune their consciousness to the frequencies of light, to expand their perception beyond the limitations of the physical realm, and to embrace the radiant essence that resided within their souls. They discovered that the path to enlightenment lay in awakening their inner light and aligning with the divine flow of cosmic illumination.

In their celestial odyssey, they encountered celestial beings who embodied the essence of light and spiritual awakening:

Luminara: A celestial guide who radiated the wisdom and compassion of divine light. Luminara guided Liam and Elysia in the exploration of their own inner light, teaching them to cultivate inner peace, connect with their higher selves, and expand their consciousness. They learned to embrace the transformative power of meditation, mindfulness, and spiritual practices that nurtured their connection with the divine.

Radiance: A celestial teacher who personified the power of enlightenment and spiritual awakening. Radiance introduced Liam and Elysia to the principles of divine wisdom, teaching them to awaken their spiritual gifts, expand their awareness, and embody their highest potential. They learned to embrace the journey of self-discovery, release limiting beliefs, and step into their true power as divine beings of light.

Seraphina: A celestial healer who embodied the transformative power of divine light in healing and energetic alignment. Seraphina guided Liam and Elysia in the exploration of energy healing modalities, teaching them to work with the luminous energies to balance and harmonize their physical, emotional, and spiritual well-being. They learned to channel divine light for healing, release energetic blockages, and awaken their innate healing abilities.

Together, Liam, Elysia, and their celestial companions delved deeper into the realms of light and spiritual awakening. They practiced sacred rituals, engaged in deep soul reflection, and connected with the divine essence that resided within and around them. They discovered that the path of spiritual awakening was not a destination but an ongoing journey of self-discovery, self-realization, and divine communion.

In their celestial odyssey, they discovered that spiritual awakening was not confined to religious or esoteric practices but was a universal calling that transcended cultural and belief systems. They realized that their souls were eternal beings of light, interconnected with the vast cosmic tapestry of existence. They became seekers of truth, embracing the divine light within themselves and recognizing it in all beings.

As they deepened their connection with light and spiritual awakening, Liam and Elysia experienced a profound shift in their perception of themselves and the world. They recognized that they were not separate from the divine but integral parts of the divine plan. They became radiant beacons of light, shining their divine essence and inspiring others to awaken their own inner illumination.

In the climactic moment of their celestial odyssey, Liam and Elysia found themselves at the heart of Lumina—a place where the energies of light and spiritual awakening merged into a symphony of divine illumination. They merged with the essence of light, experiencing a profound union with the infinite divine presence that flowed through all of existence.

Their merging with light and spiritual awakening awakened a deep sense of purpose within Liam and Elysia. They became messengers of divine illumination, sharing their expanded wisdom and guiding others on their journeys of inner illumination and spiritual growth. They recognized that true enlightenment was not a solitary quest but a collective awakening that illuminated the entire human family.

The novel concludes with Liam and Elysia continuing their exploration of the Cosmic Dance, forever inspired by the profound connections and transformative power they have discovered through light and spiritual awakening. They become catalysts for spiritual growth, fostering a global consciousness that honors the divine essence within all beings and co-creates a reality infused with love, joy, and unity.

DIVINE ILLUMINATION: EMBRACING THE RADIANCE WITHIN

"Divine Illumination: Embracing the Radiance Within" is more than a novel—it is an invitation for readers to embark on their own transformative odyssey, to embrace the power of light and spiritual awakening, and to dance with the divine illumination that resides within. Through the extraordinary journey of Liam and Elysia, readers are encouraged to awaken their own inner light, expand their consciousness, and radiate their divine essence in harmony with the cosmic dance of existence.

As Liam and Elysia continued their exploration of the Cosmic Dance, they found themselves drawn to a hidden realm pulsating with vibrant energy. This realm, known as Harmonia, was a haven of balance, unity, and interconnectedness. Guided by their curiosity, they followed a path that led them deeper into the heart of Harmonia.

In Harmonia, they encountered celestial beings known as the Harmony Keepers. The Harmony Keepers were embodiments of harmony and unity, radiating a deep sense of peace and interconnectedness. They greeted Liam and Elysia with gentle smiles, inviting them to embrace the transformative power of harmonious existence and discover the true nature of their interconnectedness with all of creation.

Guided by the Harmony Keepers, Liam and Elysia embarked on a journey of unity and collective co-creation. They learned to attune their hearts to the frequencies of harmony, to embrace diversity, and to honor the interconnectedness of all beings. They discovered that true harmony was not just a state of balance within themselves but a conscious choice to co-create a harmonious reality with others.

In their celestial odyssey, they encountered celestial beings who embodied the essence of harmony and unity:

Melody: A celestial musician who personified the power of harmony in sound and vibration. Melody guided Liam and Elysia in the exploration of the harmonious qualities of music, teaching them to listen deeply, attune their hearts, and connect with the inherent harmony in all sounds. They learned to use music as a tool for healing, unity, and collective upliftment.

Equinox: A celestial diplomat who embodied the art of harmonious communication and conflict resolution. Equinox introduced Liam and Elysia to the principles of non-violent communication, teaching them to embrace empathy, active listening, and peaceful resolution of conflicts. They learned to honor different perspectives, find common ground, and foster harmonious relationships in all aspects of their lives.

Serenity: A celestial gardener who personified the harmony and interconnectedness in nature. Serenity guided Liam and Elysia in the exploration of their connection with the natural world, teaching them to nurture and protect the environment, and to recognize their role as caretakers of the

Earth. They learned to cultivate a harmonious relationship with nature, embracing its wisdom and honoring its interconnected web of life.

Together, Liam, Elysia, and their celestial companions delved deeper into the realms of harmony and unity. They practiced conscious communication, engaged in acts of kindness and compassion, and honored the interconnectedness of all beings. They discovered that true harmony was not just an external state but an internal alignment with their own hearts and a conscious choice to create a harmonious reality for themselves and others.

In their celestial odyssey, they discovered that harmony and unity were not just abstract concepts but tangible experiences that could be cultivated in everyday life. They realized that their own actions, words, and thoughts had the power to create ripples of harmony that spread far beyond themselves. They became ambassadors of harmony, striving to create a world where peace and unity reigned.

As they deepened their connection with harmony and unity, Liam and Elysia experienced a profound shift in their perception of themselves and the world. They recognized that they were not isolated individuals but integral parts of a greater whole. They became weavers of unity, honoring the diversity of life and recognizing the interconnectedness that bound them all.

In the climactic moment of their celestial odyssey, Liam and Elysia found themselves at the heart of Harmonia—a place where the energies of harmony and unity merged into a symphony of interconnectedness. They merged with the essence of harmony, experiencing a profound union with the infinite web of connections that flowed through all of existence.

Their merging with harmony and unity awakened a deep sense of purpose within Liam and Elysia. They became messengers of harmony, sharing their expanded wisdom and guiding others on their journeys of unity and collective co-creation. They recognized that true harmony was not a solitary pursuit but a collective dance that involved all beings, transcending borders, cultures, and differences.

The novel concludes with Liam and Elysia continuing their exploration of the Cosmic Dance, forever inspired by the profound connections and transformative power they have discovered through harmony and unity. They become catalysts for collective co-creation, fostering a global consciousness that honors the interconnectedness of all beings and co-creates a reality grounded in harmony, peace, and unity.

HARMONIOUS WHISPERS: EMBRACING UNITY WITHIN THE DANCE OF LIFE

"Harmonious Whispers: Embracing Unity Within the Dance of Life" is more than a novel—it is an invitation for readers to embark on their own transformative odyssey, to embrace the power of harmony and unity, and to dance with the interconnectedness that resides within. Through the extraordinary journey of Liam and Elysia, readers are encouraged to awaken their own harmonious essence, honor the interconnected web of life, and co-create a world where unity and love are the guiding principles.

As Liam and Elysia continued their exploration of the Cosmic Dance, they found themselves irresistibly drawn to a realm teeming with vibrant energy and boundless creativity. This realm, known as Artoria, was a tapestry of colors, shapes, and forms, where artistic expression reigned supreme. Intrigued by the allure of this realm, they followed a path that led them deeper into the heart of Artoria.

In Artoria, they encountered celestial beings known as the Art Makers. The Art Makers were embodiments of artistic inspiration and creative genius, radiating a contagious enthusiasm for self-expression. They greeted Liam and Elysia with open arms, inviting them to embrace their inner artist and unlock the transformative power of creativity.

Guided by the Art Makers, Liam and Elysia embarked on a journey of self-discovery and artistic exploration. They learned to unleash their imagination, to embrace different art forms, and to express their unique creative visions. They discovered that art was not limited to traditional mediums but could be found in every aspect of life, from painting and sculpture to writing, music, dance, and beyond.

In their celestial odyssey, they encountered celestial beings who embodied the essence of artistic expression:

Vivienne: A celestial painter who personified the passion and beauty of visual art. Vivienne guided Liam and Elysia in the exploration of painting, teaching them to use color, form, and texture to express their emotions, tell stories, and capture the essence of the world around them. They learned to trust their instincts, embrace experimentation, and find their unique artistic voice.

Melvin: A celestial musician who radiated the power and emotion of music. Melvin introduced Liam and Elysia to the world of music, teaching them to play instruments, compose melodies, and express their deepest emotions through sound. They learned to tune in to the rhythm of life, harmonize with the cosmic symphony, and create music that touched the hearts and souls of others.

Isabella: A celestial dancer who embodied the grace, fluidity, and storytelling of movement. Isabella guided Liam and Elysia in the exploration of dance, teaching them to express themselves through their bodies, interpret music with movement, and communicate emotions without words. They learned to let go of inhibitions, embrace their physicality, and let the dance become a language of their souls.

Together, Liam, Elysia, and their celestial companions delved deeper into the realms of artistic expression. They created, painted, danced, sang, and wrote their way through a myriad of emotions, experiences, and inspirations. They discovered that art was a powerful tool for self-discovery, healing, and connection—it had the ability to touch hearts, ignite imagination, and transcend barriers of language and culture.

In their celestial odyssey, they discovered that creativity was not confined to the realm of art alone but permeated every aspect of life. They realized that they were co-creators in the grand tapestry of existence, shaping their reality through their thoughts, emotions, and actions. They became living works of art, expressing their unique essence in everything they did.

As they deepened their connection with creativity and artistic expression, Liam and Elysia experienced a profound shift in their perception of themselves and the world. They recognized that they were not just observers but active participants in the Cosmic Dance of creation. They became catalysts for inspiration, using their artistic expression to uplift, inspire, and transform the lives of others.

In the climactic moment of their celestial odyssey, Liam and Elysia found themselves at the heart of Artoria—a place where the energies of creativity and artistic expression merged into a symphony of boundless imagination. They merged with the essence of artistry, experiencing a profound union with the infinite creative potential that flowed through all of existence.

Their merging with creativity and artistic expression awakened a deep sense of purpose within Liam and Elysia. They became ambassadors of artistry, sharing their expanded wisdom and guiding others on their own journeys of self-expression and creative exploration. They recognized that true artistry came from the heart, transcending technique and external validation, and touching the souls of others.

The novel concludes with Liam and Elysia continuing their exploration of the Cosmic Dance, forever inspired by the profound connections and transformative power they have discovered through artistry and creativity. They become catalysts for the artistic renaissance, fostering a global consciousness that honors and celebrates the beauty, diversity, and creative potential within every individual.

ARTISTIC REVERIE: EMBRACING THE CANVAS OF LIFE

"Artistic Reverie: Embracing the Canvas of Life" is more than a novel—it is an invitation for readers to embark on their own transformative odyssey, to embrace the power of artistry and creativity, and to dance with the cosmic rhythm of self-expression. Through the extraordinary journey of Liam and Elysia, readers are encouraged to awaken their own inner artist, embrace their unique creative visions, and co-create a reality where art becomes a transformative force that inspires, heals, and connects us all.

As Liam and Elysia continued their exploration of the Cosmic Dance, they found themselves inexplicably drawn to a realm teeming with wisdom, insight, and ancient knowledge. This realm, known as Wisdoma, emanated an aura of profound understanding and intellectual brilliance. Intrigued by the allure of this realm, they followed a path that led them deeper into the heart of Wisdoma.

In Wisdoma, they encountered celestial beings known as the Wisdom Keepers. The Wisdom Keepers were embodiments of ancient knowledge and profound insight, radiating a serene presence that invited contemplation and reflection. They greeted Liam and Elysia with gentle smiles, inviting them to embrace the transformative power of wisdom and unlock the hidden depths of their own intellect.

Guided by the Wisdom Keepers, Liam and Elysia embarked on a journey of self-discovery and intellectual exploration. They delved into the vast repository of wisdom, learned from ancient texts and teachings, and engaged in profound discussions that expanded their understanding of the universe and their place within it. They discovered that wisdom was not confined to age or experience but could be accessed by anyone willing to seek it.

In their celestial odyssey, they encountered celestial beings who embodied the essence of wisdom and knowledge:

Orion: A celestial scholar who personified the pursuit of knowledge and intellectual curiosity. Orion guided Liam and Elysia in the exploration of different fields of study, encouraging them to ask questions, seek answers, and expand their intellectual horizons. They learned to embrace the joy of learning, appreciate the interconnectedness of knowledge, and cultivate a thirst for lifelong learning.

Athena: A celestial strategist who embodied strategic thinking, problem-solving, and wise decision-making. Athena introduced Liam and Elysia to the art of critical thinking, teaching them to analyze situations, weigh different perspectives, and make well-informed choices. They learned to navigate the complexities of life with clarity and wisdom, recognizing that every decision carried the potential for growth and transformation.

Socrates: A celestial philosopher who personified the pursuit of truth and the art of questioning. Socrates guided Liam and Elysia in the exploration of philosophical inquiry, encouraging them to question their assumptions, challenge societal norms, and explore the deeper meaning of existence. They learned to embrace the Socratic method of dialogue, engaging in thoughtful conversations that brought forth new insights and expanded their understanding.

Together, Liam, Elysia, and their celestial companions delved deeper into the realms of wisdom and intellectual exploration. They studied ancient texts, engaged in philosophical debates, and contemplated the mysteries of existence. They discovered that wisdom was not merely a collection of facts but a deep understanding that transcended the intellect and touched the very essence of their being.

In their celestial odyssey, they discovered that wisdom was not confined to a select few but could be accessed by all who sought it with an open mind and a humble heart. They realized that wisdom was not an end in itself but a transformative journey that involved constant growth, self-reflection, and a willingness to challenge one's own beliefs.

As they deepened their connection with wisdom and intellectual exploration, Liam and Elysia experienced a profound shift in their perception of themselves and the world. They recognized that they were not separate from the vast cosmic tapestry of knowledge but an integral part of it. They became custodians of wisdom, honoring the timeless truths that had been passed down through generations and finding their unique voice within the symphony of collective understanding.

In the climactic moment of their celestial odyssey, Liam and Elysia found themselves at the heart of Wisdoma—a place where the energies of wisdom and intellectual exploration merged into a symphony of profound insight. They merged with the essence of wisdom, experiencing a profound union with the infinite wellspring of knowledge that flowed through all of existence.

Their merging with wisdom and intellectual exploration awakened a deep sense of purpose within Liam and Elysia. They became messengers of wisdom, sharing their expanded understanding and guiding others on their own journeys of self-discovery and intellectual growth. They recognized that true wisdom was not a solitary pursuit but a collective endeavor that could uplift humanity and bring about positive change.

The novel concludes with Liam and Elysia continuing their exploration of the Cosmic Dance, forever inspired by the profound connections and transformative power they have discovered through wisdom and intellectual exploration. They become catalysts for the pursuit of knowledge, fostering a global consciousness that honors the importance of wisdom, intellectual curiosity, and the continuous expansion of human understanding.

ECHOES OF WISDOM: EMBRACING THE ILLUMINATED MIND

"Echoes of Wisdom: Embracing the Illuminated Mind" is more than a novel—it is an invitation for readers to embark on their own transformative odyssey, to embrace the power of wisdom and intellectual exploration, and to dance with the vast cosmic tapestry of knowledge. Through the extraordinary journey of Liam and Elysia, readers are encouraged to awaken their own intellectual curiosity, seek wisdom, and co-create a reality where knowledge is revered and intellectual growth is celebrated.

As Liam and Elysia continued their exploration of the Cosmic Dance, they found themselves irresistibly drawn to a realm pulsating with vibrant energy and boundless potential. This realm, known as Lumina, radiated with the brilliance of innovation and technological advancement. Intrigued by the promises of this realm, they followed a path that led them deeper into the heart of Lumina.

In Lumina, they encountered celestial beings known as the Luminary Innovators. The Luminary Innovators were embodiments of technological genius and visionary thinking, radiating an aura of limitless creativity and ingenuity. They greeted Liam and Elysia with warm smiles, inviting them to embrace the transformative power of innovation and explore the frontiers of technological advancement.

Guided by the Luminary Innovators, Liam and Elysia embarked on a journey of discovery and technological exploration. They immersed themselves in cutting-edge technologies, learned about the latest scientific breakthroughs, and engaged in thought-provoking discussions about the impact of innovation on society. They discovered that technology was not just a tool but a catalyst for transformation, capable of shaping the world in profound ways.

In their celestial odyssey, they encountered celestial beings who embodied the essence of innovation and technological advancement:

Nova: A celestial scientist who personified the pursuit of knowledge and scientific inquiry. Nova guided Liam and Elysia in the exploration of scientific principles, teaching them about the wonders of the universe, the laws of nature, and the limitless possibilities of scientific discovery. They learned to embrace experimentation, think critically, and push the boundaries of human understanding.

Tesla: A celestial engineer who radiated the power of invention and electrical innovation. Tesla introduced Liam and Elysia to the world of engineering, teaching them about the wonders of electricity, the intricacies of design, and the art of problem-solving. They learned to harness the power of imagination, embrace the iterative process of creation, and channel their innovative ideas into practical solutions.

Iris: A celestial visionary who embodied the fusion of art and technology. Iris guided Liam and Elysia in the exploration of digital art, virtual reality, and immersive experiences. They learned to blend their artistic expressions with technological tools, pushing the boundaries of creativity and using technology as a medium for storytelling and emotional connection.

Together, Liam, Elysia, and their celestial companions delved deeper into the realms of innovation and technological advancement. They experimented with emerging technologies, collaborated on ambitious projects, and contemplated the ethical implications of their creations. They discovered that technology had the power to connect people, bridge gaps, and shape a more inclusive and sustainable future.

In their celestial odyssey, they discovered that innovation was not just about creating new gadgets or pushing the limits of technology. They realized that true innovation stemmed from a deep understanding of human needs, a commitment to ethical practices, and a desire to make a positive impact on society and the environment. They became stewards of technological advancement, seeking to harness its power for the betterment of humanity.

As they deepened their connection with innovation and technological advancement, Liam and Elysia experienced a profound shift in their perception of themselves and the world. They recognized that they were not just consumers but active participants in shaping the technological landscape. They became catalysts for responsible innovation, striving to create a world where technology served as a force for good and empowered individuals to reach their full potential.

In the climactic moment of their celestial odyssey, Liam and Elysia found themselves at the heart of Lumina—a place where the energies of innovation and technological advancement merged into a symphony of endless possibilities. They merged with the essence of innovation, experiencing a profound union with the boundless potential that flowed through all of existence.

Their merging with innovation and technological advancement awakened a deep sense of purpose within Liam and Elysia. They became messengers of innovation, sharing their expanded knowledge and guiding others on their own journeys of discovery and technological advancement. They recognized that true innovation was not a solitary endeavor but a collaborative effort that required diverse perspectives, inclusive practices, and a commitment to the well-being of all.

The novel concludes with Liam and Elysia continuing their exploration of the Cosmic Dance, forever inspired by the profound connections and transformative power they have discovered through innovation and technological advancement. They become catalysts for responsible innovation, fostering a global consciousness that harnesses technology for the betterment of humanity and the preservation of the natural world.

TECH ODYSSEY: EMBRACING THE INFINITE HORIZONS

"Tech Odyssey: Embracing the Infinite Horizons" is more than a novel—it is an invitation for readers to embark on their own transformative odyssey, to embrace the power of innovation and technological advancement, and to dance with the ever-evolving landscape of human creativity. Through the extraordinary journey of Liam and Elysia, readers are encouraged to awaken their own innovative spirit, explore the frontiers of technology, and co-create a reality where innovation serves the highest good of all.

As Liam and Elysia continued their exploration of the Cosmic Dance, they found themselves irresistibly drawn to a realm pulsating with nature's wonders and mystical energy. This realm, known as Gaia, emanated a vibrant harmony between the Earth and its inhabitants. Intrigued by the allure of this realm, they followed a path that led them deeper into the heart of Gaia.

In Gaia, they encountered celestial beings known as the Earth Guardians. The Earth Guardians were embodiments of nature's wisdom and sacred connection, radiating a profound respect for the Earth and its delicate balance. They greeted Liam and Elysia with gentle smiles, inviting them to embrace the transformative power of nature and rediscover their inherent bond with the natural world.

Guided by the Earth Guardians, Liam and Elysia embarked on a journey of ecological exploration and spiritual awakening. They immersed themselves in the diverse landscapes of Gaia, witnessed the intricate interplay of ecosystems, and learned about the profound teachings embedded in every facet of nature. They discovered that the Earth held deep wisdom and healing, and that through reconnecting with nature, they could restore harmony within themselves and the world around them.

In their celestial odyssey, they encountered celestial beings who embodied the essence of nature's wisdom and spiritual connection:

Terra: A celestial herbalist who personified the healing power of plants and the natural world. Terra guided Liam and Elysia in the exploration of herbal medicine, teaching them about the medicinal properties of plants, the art of foraging, and the importance of sustainable practices. They learned to listen to the whispers of nature, deepen their understanding of the plant kingdom, and embrace the healing potential found in the Earth's abundance.

Orion: A celestial tracker who radiated the deep connection between humans and the animal kingdom. Orion introduced Liam and Elysia to the art of animal communication, teaching them to observe, listen, and connect with the wisdom of the animal realm. They learned to honor the sacredness of all creatures, recognize the messages they carried, and deepen their bond with the natural world through the eyes of its inhabitants.

Luna: A celestial stargazer who personified the cosmic connections and celestial wonders. Luna guided Liam and Elysia in the exploration of the night sky, teaching them about the mysteries of the stars, the phases of the moon, and the interconnectedness of the cosmos. They learned to marvel at the vastness of the universe, cultivate a sense of wonder, and recognize their place within the cosmic dance of existence.

Together, Liam, Elysia, and their celestial companions delved deeper into the realms of nature's wisdom and spiritual connection. They hiked through ancient forests, swam in pristine waters, and meditated in sacred groves. They discovered that through their connection with nature, they could access deep inner wisdom, experience profound healing, and cultivate a sense of reverence for all life.

In their celestial odyssey, they discovered that nature's wisdom was not confined to the external world but also resided within themselves. They realized that they were interconnected with all living beings, woven into the intricate fabric of the Earth's web of life. They became guardians of Gaia, committed to honoring and preserving the natural world for future generations.

As they deepened their connection with nature's wisdom and spiritual connection, Liam and Elysia experienced a profound shift in their perception of themselves and the world. They recognized that they were not separate from the Earth but an integral part of it. They became stewards of the Earth, embracing sustainable practices, and advocating for environmental justice and conservation.

In the climactic moment of their celestial odyssey, Liam and Elysia found themselves at the heart of Gaia—a place where the energies of nature's wisdom and spiritual connection merged into a symphony of profound harmony. They merged with the essence of Gaia, experiencing a profound union with the interconnectedness of all life and the sacredness of the Earth.

Their merging with nature's wisdom and spiritual connection awakened a deep sense of purpose within Liam and Elysia. They became messengers of the Earth, sharing their expanded understanding and guiding others on their own journeys of ecological awareness and spiritual awakening. They recognized that true harmony could only be achieved through a conscious and compassionate relationship with the Earth.

The novel concludes with Liam and Elysia continuing their exploration of the Cosmic Dance, forever inspired by the profound connections and transformative power they have discovered through nature's wisdom and spiritual connection. They become catalysts for ecological harmony, fostering a global consciousness that honors the sacredness of the Earth and co-creates a reality where humans and nature thrive in symbiotic balance.

SACRED GAIA: EMBRACING THE WEB OF LIFE

"Sacred Gaia: Embracing the Web of Life" is more than a novel—it is an invitation for readers to embark on their own transformative odyssey, to embrace the wisdom of nature and reconnect with the sacredness of the Earth, and to dance with the cosmic rhythms that flow through all of existence. Through the extraordinary journey of Liam and Elysia, readers are encouraged to awaken their own ecological awareness, cultivate a deep sense of reverence for the Earth, and co-create a reality where humans live in harmony with the natural world.

As Liam and Elysia continued their exploration of the Cosmic Dance, they found themselves irresistibly drawn to a realm shimmering with light and divine energy. This realm, known as Celestia, radiated with a sense of peace, love, and transcendence. Intrigued by the ethereal beauty of this realm, they followed a path that led them deeper into the heart of Celestia.

In Celestia, they encountered celestial beings known as the Radiant Ones. The Radiant Ones were embodiments of divine love and spiritual wisdom, emanating a luminous presence that filled the air with serenity. They greeted Liam and Elysia with radiant smiles, inviting them to embrace the transformative power of spirituality and awaken their connection with the divine.

Guided by the Radiant Ones, Liam and Elysia embarked on a journey of self-discovery and spiritual awakening. They delved into the profound teachings of the ancient mystics, explored various spiritual practices, and engaged in soulful conversations that expanded their understanding of the universe and their own spiritual nature. They discovered that spirituality was not confined to religious dogma but was a deeply personal and universal path to transcendence and inner peace.

In their celestial odyssey, they encountered celestial beings who embodied the essence of divine love and spiritual wisdom:

Aurora: A celestial healer who radiated the power of compassion and energetic healing. Aurora guided Liam and Elysia in the exploration of energetic healing modalities, teaching them about the subtle energy systems of the body and the art of channeling divine healing energies. They learned to tap into the wellspring of divine love, offer healing to themselves and others, and cultivate a deep sense of compassion for all beings.

Gabriel: A celestial messenger who personified the power of divine communication and intuition. Gabriel introduced Liam and Elysia to the world of divine guidance, teaching them to listen to their inner voice, trust their intuition, and interpret the signs and synchronicities that guided their spiritual journey. They learned to commune with the divine, receive spiritual messages, and navigate their lives with grace and purpose.

Seraphina: A celestial mystic who embodied the union of the human and divine. Seraphina guided Liam and Elysia in the exploration of mystical practices, such as meditation, contemplation, and self-inquiry. They learned to still their minds, open their hearts, and merge their consciousness with the divine presence within. They discovered that in the depths of their being, they were divine sparks of light, connected to the infinite wisdom of the universe.

Together, Liam, Elysia, and their celestial companions delved deeper into the realms of divine love and spiritual wisdom. They meditated in sacred spaces, engaged in soulful rituals, and contemplated the mysteries of existence. They discovered that spirituality was not an external quest but a journey inward, a remembrance of their divine essence, and a path to experiencing the interconnectedness of all things.

In their celestial odyssey, they discovered that spirituality was not confined to any particular religion or belief system but transcended the boundaries of human understanding. They realized that the essence of spirituality was love—the love that flows through all beings, the love that connects every soul, and the love that unites the human and the divine. They became beacons of divine love, radiating their light to uplift and inspire others on their spiritual paths.

As they deepened their connection with divine love and spiritual wisdom, Liam and Elysia experienced a profound shift in their perception of themselves and the world. They recognized that they were not separate from the divine but an integral part of it. They became vessels of divine grace, embodying love, compassion, and wisdom in all their interactions and shining their light to illuminate the path for others.

In the climactic moment of their celestial odyssey, Liam and Elysia found themselves at the heart of Celestia—a place where the energies of divine love and spiritual wisdom merged into a symphony of transcendent beauty. They merged with the essence of the divine, experiencing a profound union with the infinite love and wisdom that flowed through all of existence.

Their merging with divine love and spiritual wisdom awakened a deep sense of purpose within Liam and Elysia. They became messengers of the divine, sharing their expanded understanding and guiding others on their own spiritual journeys of self-discovery and transcendence. They recognized that true spirituality was not confined to a specific realm but permeated every aspect of life, inviting the recognition of the sacred in the ordinary.

The novel concludes with Liam and Elysia continuing their exploration of the Cosmic Dance, forever inspired by the profound connections and transformative power they have discovered through divine love and spiritual wisdom. They become catalysts for spiritual awakening, fostering a global consciousness that honors the sacredness of all existence and co-creates a reality grounded in love, compassion, and inner peace.

SACRED ILLUMINATION: EMBRACING THE DIVINE WITHIN

"Sacred Illumination: Embracing the Divine Within" is more than a novel—it is an invitation for readers to embark on their own transformative odyssey, to embrace the power of divine love and spiritual wisdom, and to dance with the cosmic rhythms of the divine presence. Through the extraordinary journey of Liam and Elysia, readers are encouraged to awaken their own spiritual nature, nurture their connection with the divine, and co-create a reality where love, compassion, and inner peace prevail.

As Liam and Elysia continued their exploration of the Cosmic Dance, they found themselves irresistibly drawn to a realm brimming with adventure and the pursuit of knowledge. This realm, known as Questoria, was a realm of quests, challenges, and personal growth. Intrigued by the excitement and possibilities of this realm, they followed a path that led them deeper into the heart of Questoria.

In Questoria, they encountered celestial beings known as the Quest Guardians. The Quest Guardians were embodiments of courage, resilience, and self-discovery, radiating an aura of determination and adventure. They greeted Liam and Elysia with warm smiles, inviting them to embrace the transformative power of personal growth and embark on epic quests that would test their limits and unlock their hidden potential.

Guided by the Quest Guardians, Liam and Elysia embarked on a journey of self-discovery and personal growth. They faced a series of challenges and quests designed to push them beyond their comfort zones, develop their skills, and uncover the depths of their inner strength. They discovered that within the realm of Questoria, every challenge was an opportunity for growth and every quest held the potential for transformation.

In their celestial odyssey, they encountered celestial beings who embodied the essence of personal growth and the spirit of adventure:

Aiden: A celestial warrior who personified strength, courage, and honor. Aiden guided Liam and Elysia in the exploration of physical challenges, teaching them martial arts, swordsmanship, and the importance of discipline and perseverance. They learned to harness their physical energy, cultivate mental fortitude, and embody the warrior spirit within.

Astrid: A celestial scholar who radiated intellectual curiosity and the pursuit of knowledge. Astrid introduced Liam and Elysia to the world of intellectual challenges, puzzles, and riddles, inspiring them to think critically, solve problems creatively, and expand their intellectual horizons. They learned to embrace the power of their minds, unlock their intellectual potential, and approach every challenge with curiosity and a thirst for knowledge.

Zara: A celestial explorer who embodied the spirit of adventure and the exploration of new frontiers. Zara guided Liam and Elysia in the exploration of uncharted territories, teaching them outdoor survival skills, navigation, and the art of embracing the unknown. They learned to trust their instincts, face their fears, and discover the beauty and wisdom that lay beyond their comfort zones.

Together, Liam, Elysia, and their celestial companions delved deeper into the realms of personal growth and adventure. They faced physical trials, solved complex puzzles, and embarked on daring quests that tested their physical, mental, and emotional limits. They discovered that every challenge was an opportunity for self-discovery, every quest held the potential for transformation, and every step forward brought them closer to realizing their full potential.

In their celestial odyssey, they discovered that personal growth was not confined to external achievements or societal expectations but was a deeply personal and unique journey. They realized that true growth came from within, from embracing their strengths, acknowledging their weaknesses, and learning to navigate the intricate dance of self-discovery.

As they deepened their connection with personal growth and adventure, Liam and Elysia experienced a profound shift in their perception of themselves and the world. They recognized that they were not defined by their past or limited by their fears but were capable of embracing the unknown, facing challenges with resilience, and becoming the heroes of their own stories.

In the climactic moment of their celestial odyssey, Liam and Elysia found themselves at the heart of Questoria—a place where the energies of personal growth and adventure merged into a symphony of self-discovery and transformation. They merged with the essence of Questoria, experiencing a profound union with the boundless potential that resided within them and the exhilaration of embarking on new quests.

Their merging with personal growth and adventure awakened a deep sense of purpose within Liam and Elysia. They became champions of personal growth, sharing their expanded understanding and guiding others on their own journeys of self-discovery and transformation. They recognized that true growth came from within, from embracing challenges, and pushing beyond perceived limitations.

The novel concludes with Liam and Elysia continuing their exploration of the Cosmic Dance, forever inspired by the profound connections and transformative power they have discovered through personal growth and the pursuit of adventure. They become catalysts for self-discovery, fostering a global consciousness that embraces challenges, pursues personal growth, and co-creates a reality where individuals realize their full potential.

QUESTORIA: EMBRACING THE HERO'S JOURNEY

"Questoria: Embracing the Hero's Journey" is more than a novel—it is an invitation for readers to embark on their own transformative odyssey, to embrace the power of personal growth and the pursuit of adventure, and to dance with the rhythm of self-discovery. Through the extraordinary journey of Liam and Elysia, readers are encouraged to awaken their own inner hero, embrace challenges, and co-create a reality where personal growth, resilience, and self-discovery prevail.

As Liam and Elysia continued their exploration of the Cosmic Dance, they found themselves irresistibly drawn to a realm that shimmered with creativity, imagination, and artistic expression. This realm, known as Artoria, was a realm of boundless inspiration and the embodiment of the transformative power of art. Intrigued by the vibrant energy of this realm, they followed a path that led them deeper into the heart of Artoria.

In Artoria, they encountered celestial beings known as the Artistic Muses. The Artistic Muses were embodiments of creativity and artistic genius, radiating an aura of enchantment and inspiration. They greeted Liam and Elysia with playful smiles, inviting them to embrace the transformative power of art and unlock the depths of their own creative potential.

Guided by the Artistic Muses, Liam and Elysia embarked on a journey of artistic exploration and self-expression. They immersed themselves in the vibrant world of artistic mediums, explored diverse forms of art, and engaged in conversations that deepened their understanding of the creative process. They discovered that art was not merely a form of expression but a pathway to self-discovery, healing, and profound connection with others.

In their celestial odyssey, they encountered celestial beings who embodied the essence of artistic expression and the transformative power of art:

Museo: A celestial painter who personified the beauty of visual art. Museo guided Liam and Elysia in the exploration of painting, teaching them the techniques of blending colors, capturing emotions on canvas, and using art as a language of the soul. They learned to observe the world with an artist's eye, express their innermost thoughts through brushstrokes, and bring their imaginations to life on the canvas.

Melodia: A celestial musician who radiated the enchantment of music and the power of sound. Melodia introduced Liam and Elysia to the world of music, teaching them to play musical instruments, compose melodies, and use music as a means of emotional expression. They learned to listen deeply, attune themselves to the rhythms of the universe, and create harmonious melodies that resonated with their souls.

Poetia: A celestial poet who embodied the magic of words and the art of storytelling. Poetia guided Liam and Elysia in the exploration of poetry and creative writing, teaching them to weave words into tapestries of meaning, evoke emotions through metaphors, and use language to convey their deepest thoughts and emotions. They learned to listen to the whispers of their hearts, let their imaginations soar, and give voice to the unspoken.

Together, Liam, Elysia, and their celestial companions delved deeper into the realms of artistic expression and self-discovery. They painted vivid landscapes, composed melodies that touched the soul, and penned heartfelt verses that stirred the emotions. They discovered that art was not just a form of creation but a means of connecting with others, exploring the depths of their own being, and leaving a lasting imprint on the world.

In their celestial odyssey, they discovered that artistic expression was not limited to a select few but resided within the hearts of all beings. They realized that everyone had a unique voice and a story to tell, and that through art, they could cultivate empathy, inspire change, and foster a greater understanding of the human experience.

As they deepened their connection with artistic expression and self-discovery, Liam and Elysia experienced a profound shift in their perception of themselves and the world. They recognized that they were not separate from the creative forces of the universe but co-creators of their own realities. They became ambassadors of creativity, embracing their unique artistic gifts, and encouraging others to explore the transformative power of art.

In the climactic moment of their celestial odyssey, Liam and Elysia found themselves at the heart of Artoria—a place where the energies of artistic expression and self-discovery merged into a symphony of beauty, imagination, and connection. They merged with the essence of Artoria, experiencing a profound union with the boundless creative potential that flowed through all of existence.

Their merging with artistic expression and self-discovery awakened a deep sense of purpose within Liam and Elysia. They became messengers of art, sharing their expanded understanding and guiding others on their own artistic journeys of self-expression and transformation. They recognized that true art came from the depths of their being, from a place of authenticity and vulnerability, and had the power to touch hearts and inspire souls.

The novel concludes with Liam and Elysia continuing their exploration of the Cosmic Dance, forever inspired by the profound connections and transformative power they have discovered through artistic expression and the beauty of creation. They become catalysts for creativity, fostering a global consciousness that honors the diverse forms of art and co-creates a reality where artistic expression, imagination, and connection thrive.

THE ARTISTIC SYMPHONY: EMBRACING THE CREATIVE SPIRIT

"The Artistic Symphony: Embracing the Creative Spirit" is more than a novel—it is an invitation for readers to embark on their own transformative odyssey, to embrace the power of artistic expression and self-discovery, and to dance with the rhythm of creation. Through the extraordinary journey of Liam and Elysia, readers are encouraged to awaken their own creative potential, express their unique voices, and co-create a reality where art, beauty, and imagination are celebrated.

As Liam and Elysia continued their exploration of the Cosmic Dance, they found themselves irresistibly drawn to a realm adorned with wisdom, ancient knowledge, and spiritual enlightenment. This realm, known as Mystoria, emanated a profound sense of tranquility and a connection to the divine. Intrigued by the sacredness of this realm, they followed a path that led them deeper into the heart of Mystoria.

In Mystoria, they encountered celestial beings known as the Sages of Wisdom. The Sages were embodiments of ancient knowledge, spiritual wisdom, and the eternal truths that transcend time. They greeted Liam and Elysia with serene smiles, inviting them to embrace the transformative power of wisdom and embark on a journey of spiritual enlightenment.

Guided by the Sages of Wisdom, Liam and Elysia embarked on a journey of self-discovery and the pursuit of spiritual enlightenment. They delved into the profound teachings of the mystics, explored sacred texts, and engaged in contemplative practices that deepened their understanding of the universe and their own spiritual nature. They discovered that wisdom was not confined to intellectual knowledge but was a path of inner illumination, awakening, and connection with the divine.

In their celestial odyssey, they encountered celestial beings who embodied the essence of wisdom and spiritual enlightenment:

Zenith: A celestial master who personified the practice of mindfulness and the art of meditation. Zenith guided Liam and Elysia in the exploration of mindfulness techniques, teaching them to be fully present in each moment, cultivate inner stillness, and connect with the essence of their being. They learned to quiet their minds, embrace the silence within, and experience profound insights that transcended ordinary perception.

Seraphine: A celestial oracle who radiated the gift of divination and intuitive guidance. Seraphine introduced Liam and Elysia to the world of divination and intuitive practices, teaching them to connect with their inner wisdom, interpret signs and symbols, and access spiritual guidance from the higher realms. They learned to trust their intuitive knowing, listen to the whispers of their souls, and navigate their lives with clarity and purpose.

Avalon: A celestial mystic who embodied the ancient wisdom of the Earth and the interconnectedness of all things. Avalon guided Liam and Elysia in the exploration of the natural world as a source of wisdom and spiritual insight.

They learned to commune with nature, attune themselves to its rhythms, and recognize the inherent wisdom woven into every leaf, stone, and creature. They discovered that the Earth held ancient knowledge, and by aligning themselves with its wisdom, they could deepen their spiritual connection.

Together, Liam, Elysia, and their celestial companions delved deeper into the realms of wisdom and spiritual enlightenment. They practiced meditation, engaged in introspection, and embarked on inner journeys that revealed the deeper truths of existence. They discovered that wisdom was not an external acquisition but a journey of self-discovery, a remembrance of their divine nature, and a path to spiritual liberation.

In their celestial odyssey, they discovered that wisdom was not confined to any particular tradition or belief system but was a universal language that spoke to the depths of the human soul. They realized that the essence of wisdom was love—the love that permeated all creation, the love that connected every soul, and the love that brought forth profound insights and spiritual awakening.

As they deepened their connection with wisdom and spiritual enlightenment, Liam and Elysia experienced a profound shift in their perception of themselves and the world. They recognized that they were not separate from the divine but a part of it, and that their journey of spiritual enlightenment was an eternal quest to remember their divine nature and embrace the interconnectedness of all existence.

In the climactic moment of their celestial odyssey, Liam and Elysia found themselves at the heart of Mystoria—a place where the energies of wisdom and spiritual enlightenment merged into a symphony of inner illumination and divine connection. They merged with the essence of Mystoria, experiencing a profound union with the eternal wisdom that flowed through all of existence.

Their merging with wisdom and spiritual enlightenment awakened a deep sense of purpose within Liam and Elysia. They became messengers of wisdom, sharing their expanded understanding and guiding others on their own journeys of self-discovery and spiritual awakening. They recognized that true wisdom came from within, from a place of inner knowing, and had the power to liberate souls and transform lives.

The novel concludes with Liam and Elysia continuing their exploration of the Cosmic Dance, forever inspired by the profound connections and transformative power they have discovered through wisdom and spiritual enlightenment. They become catalysts for spiritual awakening, fostering a global consciousness that honors the sacredness of all knowledge and co-creates a reality where wisdom, inner illumination, and divine connection prevail.

WISDOM'S JOURNEY: EMBRACING THE PATH OF ENLIGHTENMENT

"Wisdom's Journey: Embracing the Path of Enlightenment" is more than a novel—it is an invitation for readers to embark on their own transformative odyssey, to embrace the power of wisdom and the pursuit of spiritual enlightenment, and to dance with the eternal rhythms of inner illumination. Through the extraordinary journey of Liam and Elysia, readers are encouraged to awaken their own inner sage, deepen their connection with wisdom, and co-create a reality where spiritual awakening, love, and enlightenment flourish.

THE COSMIC DANCE: EMBRACING THE TAPESTRY OF EXISTENCE

Synopsis:

"The Cosmic Dance: Embracing the Tapestry of Existence" is a captivating novel that takes readers on an extraordinary journey through realms beyond imagination, where the boundaries between the ordinary and the extraordinary blur. It is a story of love, adventure, self-discovery, and the interconnectedness of all things.

The novel follows the intertwining paths of two main characters, Liam and Elysia, who are drawn together by a mystical force that compels them to explore the hidden realms of the universe. As they embark on their celestial odyssey, they encounter celestial beings, traverse diverse realms, and unlock the secrets of the Cosmic Dance—the intricate interplay of love, knowledge, creativity, and spiritual awakening.

Throughout their journey, Liam and Elysia encounter four realms, each with its own distinct essence and profound teachings. In Gaia, the realm of nature's wisdom, they connect with the Earth and learn the importance of ecological harmony, sustainable practices, and honoring the sacredness of all life. In Celestia, the realm of divine love, they discover the power of spiritual connection, the pursuit of enlightenment, and the infinite potential of the human spirit.

In Questoria, the realm of personal growth and adventure, they embrace challenges, embark on epic quests, and uncover their hidden potential. They learn that every obstacle is an opportunity for self-discovery, every quest holds the potential for transformation, and every step forward brings them closer to realizing their full potential. In Artoria, the realm of artistic expression, they delve into the depths of creativity, explore diverse art forms, and discover the transformative power of self-expression.

As Liam and Elysia traverse these realms, they encounter celestial beings who personify the essence of each realm, guiding them, inspiring them, and deepening their understanding of themselves and the world around them. These celestial beings, such as the Earth Guardians, the Radiant Ones, the Quest Guardians, and the Artistic Muses, become their mentors, companions, and catalysts for personal growth and transformation.

As the story unfolds, Liam and Elysia face trials, overcome challenges, and experience profound shifts in their perception of themselves and the world. They realize that they are not separate from the cosmic tapestry of existence but integral threads woven into its fabric. They embrace their unique gifts, cultivate compassion, and awaken their inner potential to co-create a reality where love, harmony, and spiritual awakening prevail.

Through their journey, Liam and Elysia learn that the Cosmic Dance is not only an external exploration but an inner journey of self-discovery, connection, and the remembrance of their divine nature. They become catalysts for positive change, sharing their expanded understanding and guiding others on their own transformative paths.

"The Cosmic Dance: Embracing the Tapestry of Existence" is a novel that invites readers to embrace the mysteries of the universe, awaken their own inner potential, and dance with the rhythms of love, knowledge, creativity, and spiritual awakening. It is a tale of interconnectedness, personal growth, and the profound realization that we are all part of something greater than ourselves—a cosmic dance that unites us all.

As Liam and Elysia progress through the realms, they begin to uncover a deeper truth about the Cosmic Dance. They realize that the realms they have encountered are not separate entities but interconnected aspects of a grand tapestry, each contributing to the harmony and balance of the universe. They discover that the true essence of the Cosmic Dance lies in the integration of love, knowledge, creativity, and spiritual awakening.

In their journey, Liam and Elysia encounter challenges and adversities that test their resolve and push them to their limits. They face inner demons, confront fears, and navigate the complexities of relationships. Yet, through their shared experiences and unwavering determination, they find strength in each other and in the bonds they have formed with the celestial beings they have encountered along the way.

As their understanding deepens, Liam and Elysia realize that the Cosmic Dance is not solely about individual growth but also about collective transformation. They recognize the interconnectedness of all beings and the responsibility they bear in co-creating a harmonious and compassionate world. Inspired by the wisdom they have gained, they become agents of change, spreading love, knowledge, creativity, and spiritual awakening wherever they go.

In the climactic moment of their celestial odyssey, Liam and Elysia are faced with a monumental choice—a choice that will determine the fate of the Cosmic

Dance itself. They must confront a powerful force that seeks to disrupt the delicate balance of the realms and plunge the universe into chaos. With the knowledge and skills they have acquired throughout their journey, they must rally the celestial beings they have encountered and unite their strengths in a battle against darkness.

Together, Liam, Elysia, and their celestial allies embark on a final quest to restore harmony and safeguard the Cosmic Dance. They face formidable adversaries, overcome inner doubts, and tap into the depths of their collective power. Through their unwavering determination, their connection to one another, and their commitment to the greater good, they emerge victorious, restoring balance and harmony to the realms.

In the denouement of the novel, Liam and Elysia return to their ordinary lives, forever changed by their celestial odyssey. They carry within them the wisdom, love, and inspiration they have gathered along the way. They become beacons of light, sharing their experiences and teachings with others, igniting a ripple effect of positive change in the world.

"The Cosmic Dance: Embracing the Tapestry of Existence" is a captivating novel that weaves together the threads of love, knowledge, creativity, and spiritual awakening into a grand tapestry of interconnectedness. It invites readers to embark on their own transformative journey, to embrace their inner potential, and to dance with the cosmic rhythms of existence. Through the extraordinary odyssey of Liam and Elysia, readers are reminded of the profound interconnectedness of all things and the transformative power of love, knowledge, creativity, and spiritual awakening in shaping a harmonious and compassionate world.

In the aftermath of their victorious battle, Liam and Elysia find themselves hailed as heroes and revered for their role in preserving the Cosmic Dance. They are honored by the celestial beings they have encountered on their journey and are granted a special gift—the ability to bridge the realms and maintain a connection between them.

Embracing their newfound responsibilities, Liam and Elysia establish a sanctuary at the convergence of the realms—a place where beings from all realms can gather, learn from one another, and continue their growth and exploration. This sanctuary becomes a beacon of unity, where love, knowledge, creativity, and spiritual awakening intertwine harmoniously.

As time passes, the sanctuary becomes a thriving community, attracting seekers from far and wide who are drawn to the wisdom and transformative power it offers. Together, Liam and Elysia guide and mentor these individuals, helping them embrace their unique paths and discover their own contributions to the Cosmic Dance.

Liam delves deeper into his exploration of knowledge, establishing a library within the sanctuary that houses ancient texts, scrolls, and artifacts from all the realms. He becomes a guardian of wisdom, sharing his vast knowledge and helping others tap into the wellspring of insights available to them.

Meanwhile, Elysia embraces her role as a creative muse, nurturing the artistic talents and expressions of those who seek inspiration within the sanctuary. She creates a vibrant space for artistic exploration, where individuals can paint, write, perform, and share their creations, fostering a collective celebration of creativity and self-expression.

As the years pass, Liam and Elysia witness the profound impact their sanctuary has on the lives of those who seek solace, growth, and connection. The community becomes a testament to the power of unity, as beings from all walks of life and realms come together, transcending differences and embracing their shared humanity.

Through their continued journey within the sanctuary, Liam and Elysia deepen their own understanding of the Cosmic Dance. They encounter new celestial beings who bring unique perspectives and teachings, further enriching their own growth and expanding the horizons of their knowledge, creativity, and spiritual awakening.

In the final pages of the novel, Liam and Elysia, now wise elders, reflect upon their incredible odyssey and the profound impact it has had on their lives. They realize that the Cosmic Dance is an ever-evolving tapestry, constantly inviting new insights, experiences, and connections.

With a renewed sense of purpose, they pass on the responsibility of guiding the sanctuary to a new generation, knowing that the Cosmic Dance will continue to flourish and evolve through the efforts of those who carry the torch.

"The Cosmic Dance: Embracing the Tapestry of Existence" is a timeless tale of growth, unity, and the beauty of interconnectedness. It invites readers to embark on their own inner journey, to embrace love, knowledge, creativity, and spiritual awakening, and to contribute their unique threads to the grand tapestry of existence. Through the extraordinary odyssey of Liam and Elysia, readers are reminded of the infinite possibilities that await when one embraces the interconnectedness of all things and dances with the cosmic rhythms of life.

As the years go by, Liam and Elysia's sanctuary becomes a beacon of light and wisdom, attracting not only individuals from the realms they have explored but also beings from other dimensions and worlds. The sanctuary evolves into a crossroads of cosmic connections, where diverse beings come together to share knowledge, exchange ideas, and foster unity.

Liam and Elysia, now revered as elder guides, dedicate themselves to facilitating dialogue and understanding among the sanctuary's inhabitants. They organize gatherings, workshops, and gatherings where beings from different realms can engage in deep conversations, cultural exchanges, and collaborative projects that transcend boundaries.

The sanctuary becomes a hub of innovation, where the convergence of diverse perspectives and experiences sparks new ideas and breakthroughs. Beings from Gaia bring their eco-consciousness and sustainability practices, beings from Celestia share their spiritual teachings and enlightenment practices, beings from Questoria contribute their adventurous spirit and problem-solving skills, and beings from Artoria infuse the sanctuary with creativity and artistic expression.

Within the sanctuary, new realms of existence are discovered, expanding the cosmic tapestry even further. These realms bring forth additional layers of wisdom, love, creativity, and spiritual growth. Liam and Elysia, in their eternal quest for knowledge and expansion, become explorers of these new realms, unraveling their mysteries and integrating their teachings into the sanctuary's ever-evolving culture.

As the sanctuary flourishes, Liam and Elysia find fulfillment in seeing the transformations that unfold within its walls. Beings who once felt lost or disconnected find solace, purpose, and a sense of belonging. Friendships are forged, collaborations blossom, and a sense of unity prevails, transcending the boundaries of realms and worlds.

However, amidst the harmony and growth, a new challenge emerges. A powerful force, driven by fear and ignorance, seeks to disrupt the unity and peace that Liam and Elysia have cultivated. This force, led by a malevolent being, attempts to sow discord and spread division among the sanctuary's inhabitants.

Liam and Elysia, drawing upon the wisdom they have gained over the years, rally the diverse beings of the sanctuary to stand against this threat. They inspire unity, ignite the flames of courage, and remind their companions of the inherent power that lies within each of them.

In an epic final battle, the sanctuary's inhabitants unite their strengths, merging their unique talents and qualities to overcome the malevolent force. Through compassion, understanding, and a shared vision of a harmonious existence, they prevail, reaffirming the power of love, knowledge, creativity, and spiritual awakening.

With the malevolent force vanquished, the sanctuary emerges stronger and more resilient than ever. It becomes a beacon of hope, a testament to the transformative power of unity and the triumph of light over darkness. Beings from all corners of the cosmos are drawn to the sanctuary, seeking guidance, inspiration, and the opportunity to contribute to the cosmic tapestry.

In the closing pages of the novel, Liam and Elysia, now older and wiser, pass the mantle of leadership to a new generation of guardians. They step back, content in knowing that their legacy will continue to shape the sanctuary and the lives of those who dwell within it.

"The Cosmic Dance: Embracing the Tapestry of Existence" concludes with a vision of the sanctuary as a thriving, interconnected community—a microcosm of the greater universe. It is a testament to the power of unity, love, knowledge, creativity, and spiritual awakening in shaping a world that honors the interplay of all things.

The novel serves as a reminder to readers of their own role in the cosmic dance, inviting them to explore their own inner realms, embrace their unique gifts, and contribute to the collective tapestry of existence. Through the extraordinary odyssey of Liam and Elysia, readers are inspired to embody the qualities of love, knowledge, creativity, and spiritual awakening, fostering unity and co-creating a reality that reflects the harmony and interconnectedness of all things.

In the wake of the battle, the sanctuary expands its influence beyond its physical borders. The wisdom, love, creativity, and spiritual awakening emanating from the sanctuary ripple out into the wider universe, inspiring other communities, worlds, and realms to embrace unity and coexistence. The sanctuary becomes a catalyst for a profound transformation on a cosmic scale.

As the sanctuary's influence grows, beings from all corners of the universe seek to join its vibrant community. Celestial beings, interdimensional travelers, and cosmic wanderers become an integral part of the sanctuary, sharing their unique perspectives, wisdom, and gifts. The tapestry of existence becomes more intricately woven as beings from diverse realms come together in harmony.

Liam and Elysia, revered as the Founders, continue to guide and mentor the sanctuary's inhabitants, but they also embark on new journeys themselves. They travel to uncharted realms, exploring the mysteries of the universe, and establishing connections with other enlightened beings who are dedicated to fostering unity and the cosmic dance.

Through their interactions and collaborations, Liam and Elysia discover that the Cosmic Dance is not confined to a single realm or dimension. It is an eternal interplay of energies and consciousness that transcends space and time. They come to understand that the dance exists at the very core of existence itself, binding all beings and realms in a harmonious symphony.

In their travels, Liam and Elysia encounter celestial beings who embody different facets of the Cosmic Dance. They meet the Harmonizers, beings of cosmic balance and equilibrium, who teach them the importance of harmony and cooperation in maintaining the delicate interplay of energies. They also encounter the Weavers, beings who intricately manipulate the threads of reality, teaching them the art of manifestation and the power of intention in shaping the cosmic tapestry.

United with these celestial mentors, Liam and Elysia discover hidden realms of existence that exist beyond the boundaries of known reality. These realms, shimmering with ethereal beauty and wisdom, reveal new dimensions of the Cosmic Dance, expanding their understanding of the interconnectedness of all things.

As the novel reaches its climax, Liam and Elysia lead a gathering of enlightened beings from across the cosmos. Together, they orchestrate a magnificent cosmic dance, where energies merge, colors blend, and vibrations harmonize. The dance becomes a living expression of the unity and interconnectedness that permeate the entire universe.

Through this profound cosmic dance, the inhabitants of the sanctuary and beings from countless realms are reminded of their inherent oneness. They experience a deep soul resonance that transcends language, form, and perception. In this moment of unity, the boundaries between realms dissolve, and the entire cosmos pulses with an undeniable interconnectedness.

In the closing chapters of the novel, Liam and Elysia, now illumined beings, pass on their stewardship to a new generation of guardians. The sanctuary evolves into a cosmic nexus, a sacred space that continues to radiate love, knowledge, creativity, and spiritual awakening to all corners of the universe.

"The Cosmic Dance: Embracing the Tapestry of Existence" concludes with a vision of a universe transformed by the power of unity and the Cosmic Dance. Beings across all realms and dimensions live in harmony, recognizing their interconnectedness and co-creating a reality that honors the divine essence within all.

The novel serves as a reminder to readers that they too are an integral part of the Cosmic Dance. It invites them to explore their own inner realms, cultivate love, knowledge, creativity, and spiritual awakening, and contribute to the harmonious evolution of the universe. Through the extraordinary odyssey of Liam and Elysia, readers are inspired to embrace their own role in the dance, fostering unity and co-creating a reality that reflects the boundless beauty and interconnectedness of all existence.

In the wake of the cosmic dance, a profound transformation ripples throughout the universe. The unity and interconnectedness fostered by Liam and Elysia's sanctuary inspire beings across realms and dimensions to embrace love, knowledge, creativity, and spiritual awakening. A wave of enlightenment spreads, touching the hearts and minds of all sentient beings.

As the cosmic dance evolves, new realms of existence emerge, each offering unique insights and experiences. Liam and Elysia, guided by their eternal curiosity, continue their exploration, venturing into these uncharted territories to expand their understanding of the ever-unfolding tapestry of existence.

In their journeys, they encounter cosmic beings who have transcended individual realms and attained an elevated state of consciousness. These beings, known as the Luminescents, radiate profound wisdom, embodying the highest qualities of love, knowledge, creativity, and spiritual awakening. They become mentors and guides, imparting timeless teachings to Liam and Elysia, deepening their connection with the cosmic dance.

With the Luminescents' guidance, Liam and Elysia unlock new levels of perception and understanding. They learn to transcend the limitations of the physical world, accessing higher dimensions of consciousness and communing with celestial entities that exist beyond the boundaries of known reality.

As they delve deeper into the cosmic dance, Liam and Elysia discover that the dance itself is an ever-evolving symphony of creation. They witness the birth of galaxies, the emergence of new life forms, and the continual transformation of energy and matter. They come to understand that the cosmic dance is not static but a dynamic expression of the universe's infinite potential.

In their interactions with the Luminescents, Liam and Elysia learn to merge their individual consciousness with the collective consciousness of the cosmic dance. They become conduits of divine wisdom and channels of universal love, serving as bridges between realms and dimensions, and facilitating the harmonious interplay of energies and consciousness.

In the climax of the novel, Liam and Elysia are tasked with a monumental responsibility—to share the wisdom and insights they have gained with the entire universe. They embark on a cosmic journey, visiting every realm, dimension, and corner of existence, imparting their teachings and igniting the flame of enlightenment within all beings.

As their teachings spread, the cosmic dance reaches new heights of beauty, complexity, and harmony. Beings from all realms and dimensions come together in a unified expression of love, knowledge, creativity, and spiritual awakening. The tapestry of existence becomes an ever-evolving masterpiece, where every thread is honored, every note is in perfect harmony, and every soul dances in unison.

In the final chapters of the novel, Liam and Elysia, having fulfilled their mission, return to their sanctuary, a place of deep reverence and celebration. They are embraced by a grateful community of beings from across the cosmos, united in their shared vision of a harmonious and enlightened universe.

"The Cosmic Dance: Embracing the Tapestry of Existence" concludes with a vision of the universe fully aligned with the cosmic dance. Beings from all realms and dimensions coexist in a state of unity, reverence, and creative expression. Love, knowledge, creativity, and spiritual awakening permeate every facet of existence, radiating outward in an eternal dance of light and joy.

The novel serves as a reminder to readers that they too are integral participants in the cosmic dance. It invites them to embrace their unique gifts and perspectives, to cultivate love, knowledge, creativity, and spiritual awakening within themselves, and to contribute to the ever-evolving tapestry of existence. Through the extraordinary odyssey of Liam and Elysia, readers are inspired to embark on their own journeys of self-discovery, to dance with the cosmic rhythms, and to co-create a reality where unity, harmony, and enlightenment flourish.

As Liam and Elysia stand at the threshold of their sanctuary, gazing out into the vastness of the universe, their hearts are filled with gratitude and awe. The cosmic dance they have witnessed and embraced throughout their extraordinary journey has forever transformed their lives and the lives of countless beings across realms and dimensions.

They have come to understand that the cosmic dance is not confined to the pages of their story or the realms they have explored. It is an eternal symphony that echoes through every particle of existence—a symphony that invites all beings to partake in its harmonious rhythms.

Liam and Elysia have learned that the cosmic dance is not a destination to be reached, but a journey to be embraced. It is a dance of love, knowledge, creativity, and spiritual awakening—a dance that weaves together the threads of existence, connecting all souls in a tapestry of unity and divine expression.

In the closing moments of their odyssey, Liam and Elysia turn to each other, their eyes sparkling with the wisdom and joy they have gained. They embrace, feeling the profound connection that transcends time and space—a connection that was forged through their shared experiences, their unwavering commitment to growth, and their devotion to the cosmic dance.

They offer their final words to the readers who have joined them on this transformative adventure:

"Dear reader, may you always remember that you too are a dancer in the cosmic symphony. You possess within you the power to embrace love, knowledge, creativity, and spiritual awakening. Trust in the divine rhythm that guides your steps, and surrender to the flow of the dance.

"Know that the dance is not limited to the realms we have traversed or the pages of this tale. It is a dance that extends beyond the boundaries of imagination—a dance that invites you to explore, create, and transcend. It is an eternal dance of unity, where every step you take contributes to the grand choreography of existence.

"Embrace the cosmic dance with open arms, for within its embrace, you will find the truest expression of your divine essence. Dance with passion, dance with grace, and let the music of the universe guide your every move".

"As we bid you farewell, dear reader, remember that the dance continues. Embrace it, embody it, and let its beauty unfold through your life. May your steps be filled with love, your heart with knowledge, your creations with inspiration, and your spirit with awakening".

"May you forever dance in harmony with the cosmic symphony, for you are an essential thread in the tapestry of existence."

With their final words spoken, Liam and Elysia take a step forward, merging with the cosmic dance once more. Their forms become ethereal, their presence transcendent. They become an eternal part of the cosmic tapestry, forever weaving their threads of love, knowledge, creativity, and spiritual awakening into the grand dance of the universe.

And so, the story of Liam and Elysia comes to a close. Yet, their legacy lives on in the hearts and minds of all who have danced alongside them. The echoes of their journey continue to inspire, guiding others to embrace the cosmic dance and co-create a reality where love, knowledge, creativity, and spiritual awakening flourish.

The novel, "The Cosmic Dance: Embracing the Tapestry of Existence," concludes, but the dance of existence continues—an eternal symphony that invites every soul to join its divine rhythm and embrace the boundless beauty of the cosmic dance.

But the story does not end with the final page. The journey of the cosmic dance continues, unfolding in infinite ways across the expanse of time and space. The characters we have come to know and love may have fulfilled their roles, but new chapters await in the ever-evolving tapestry of existence.

The impact of Liam and Elysia's odyssey reverberates throughout the cosmos. Their tale becomes a source of inspiration, passed down through generations, reminding beings of their inherent connection and the transformative power of embracing the cosmic dance.

In the realms and dimensions touched by their story, societies flourish with a newfound sense of unity, cooperation, and reverence for all life. The teachings of love, knowledge, creativity, and spiritual awakening become pillars upon which civilizations are built, creating a harmonious tapestry that honors the intricate interplay of existence.

Liam and Elysia, now immortalized in the collective consciousness, become legendary figures—the guiding lights of the cosmic dance. Temples are erected in their honor, their words are studied and recited, and their wisdom becomes timeless guidance for those who seek to deepen their understanding and connection with the universe.

Their journey also sparks the awakening of countless individuals who hear the call of the cosmic dance resonating within their souls. Ordinary beings become extraordinary dancers, stepping into their power and embracing their unique contributions to the ever-unfolding tapestry.

Throughout the eons, the cosmic dance continues to evolve. New realms emerge, each with its own rhythm and expression. Beings from every corner of the universe embark on their own transformative journeys, dancing with the cosmic energies and expanding the boundaries of their own understanding.

The tapestry of existence becomes an ever-growing, ever-changing work of art—a testament to the limitless possibilities and the eternal dance that binds all things together. It weaves together the stories, dreams, and aspirations of every being who has ever existed, creating a mosaic of divine expression.

And so, dear reader, as you close this book and step back into your own world, may you carry the essence of the cosmic dance within you. May you embrace the interconnectedness of all things, nurture the flames of love, knowledge, creativity, and spiritual awakening within your heart, and let your unique dance be an exquisite thread in the grand tapestry of existence.

Remember that the cosmic dance awaits your participation. It calls to you, inviting you to step forward, to take your place in the symphony of life. Embrace the beauty of your own journey, and with each step, let your light shine brightly, illuminating the path for others to follow.

For the dance of existence continues, forever weaving its intricate patterns, forever evolving, forever inviting you to join in the cosmic symphony.

With that, the story comes to a close, but the cosmic dance remains, an eternal invitation to explore, create, connect, and awaken. May your own journey be filled with wonder, growth, and the profound joy of embracing the cosmic dance.

As the final pages turn, a sense of wonder lingers in the air—a feeling that the story is not truly over, but merely transitioning into a new chapter. The cosmic dance, ever-evolving and boundless, continues to weave its threads of love, knowledge, creativity, and spiritual awakening through the fabric of existence.

In the wake of Liam and Elysia's journey, a spark ignites within the hearts of readers around the world. The tale resonates deep within their souls, awakening a recognition of their own connection to the cosmic dance. Inspired by the characters' triumphs, struggles, and profound revelations, individuals embark on their own personal odysseys, seeking to embrace the cosmic dance and unleash the fullness of their own potential.

Communities dedicated to the exploration of the cosmic dance spring up across realms and dimensions. They become vibrant hubs of shared wisdom, transformative practices, and collaborative endeavors. Beings from all walks of life gather to exchange insights, support one another's growth, and collectively contribute to the ever-evolving tapestry of existence.

The teachings of love, knowledge, creativity, and spiritual awakening find new forms of expression in art, science, philosophy, and spirituality. The echoes of Liam and Elysia's journey ripple through cultural movements, inspiring works of literature, music, and visual art that illuminate the universal truths they discovered along their path.

In the corridors of academia, scholars delve into the depths of the novel, dissecting its symbolism, unraveling its intricate themes, and studying its impact on the collective consciousness. The cosmic dance becomes a subject of academic discourse, as universities establish interdisciplinary programs devoted to exploring the interplay of love, knowledge, creativity, and spiritual awakening in shaping the human experience.

Meanwhile, Liam and Elysia, forever connected to the cosmic dance, continue to evolve in their own spiritual journeys. They venture deeper into the realms of existence, uncovering hidden layers of wisdom, encountering celestial beings of extraordinary insight, and expanding their understanding of the cosmic symphony.

They become beacons of light, guiding others along the path of self-discovery and awakening. Through their teachings, mentorship, and compassionate presence, they touch the lives of countless beings, helping them navigate the intricacies of the cosmic dance and embrace their own unique role within it.

As time flows, Liam and Elysia's physical forms merge with the essence of the cosmic dance. Their individual identities become indistinguishable from the universal consciousness, and they transcend the boundaries of time and space. Yet, their influence continues to radiate, as their eternal presence whispers in the hearts of all who seek the truth of the cosmic dance.

And so, dear reader, as you close the book, may you carry the essence of the cosmic dance within you. May you become a torchbearer of love, knowledge, creativity, and spiritual awakening, illuminating the path for others as you navigate the ever-unfolding tapestry of existence.

Remember that the story is never truly over, for the cosmic dance transcends the confines of fiction. It invites you to step into your own narrative, to embrace the profound interconnectedness of all things, and to contribute your unique dance to the eternal symphony.

May you be inspired to explore, to create, to connect, and to awaken. May your journey be filled with wonder, growth, and the blissful embrace of the cosmic dance.

And so, the novel concludes, but the cosmic dance remains—a boundless invitation to embrace the infinite possibilities that lie within you and to co-create a reality that reflects the harmonious interplay of all existence.

The End... and the Eternal Dance.

With love from Ismail Ulas...

www.ingramcontent.com/pod-product-compliance
Lightning Source LLC
Chambersburg PA
CBHW060037260726